Preventing HIV/AIDS in the
Middle East and North Africa

Preventing HIV/AIDS in the Middle East and North Africa

A Window of Opportunity to Act

THE WORLD BANK

Washington, D.C.

ISBN 0-8213-6264-X
e-ISBN 0-8213-6265-8
EAN 978-0-8213-6264-8
DOI 10.1596/978-0-8213-6264-8

Library of Congress Cataloging-in-Publication data has been applied for.

Contents

Acknowledgments

This strategy was prepared by a team led by Francisca Ayodeji Akala, who together with Carol Jenkins (World Bank Consultant) were the main authors. Other members of the team include Bachir Souhlal, Sameh El-Saharty, Tiguist Fisseha, and M. Yaa Pokua Afriyie Oppong. Annex 1 of the strategy was prepared by Rene Bonnel. The Health Team of the Human Development Sector, Middle East and North Africa (MENA) Region, including Akiko Maeda (MENA Health, Nutrition, and Population Sector Manager), provided significant inputs that enriched the strategy. Michal Rutkowski (MNSHD Director) provided inputs and endorsed the strategy, and Mustapha K. Nabli (MENA Chief Economist and MNSED Director) provided significant guidance and oversight throughout the preparation process. The peer reviewers were Susan Stout (Manager, World Bank Results Secretariat), Keith Hansen (Manager, ActAfrica, World Bank), Oussama Tawil (Joint United Nations Program on HIV/AIDS [UNAIDS] MENA Regional Coordinator), and Meskerem Grunitzky-Bekele (UNAIDS). Various other World Bank colleagues were consulted and provided their feedback, including Olusoji Adeyi, Osman S. Ahmed, Jacques Baudouy, Michael Borowitz, Muge M. Finkel, Subhash K. Hira, Monica Larrieu, Joan MacNeil, David Robalino, George Schieber, David Wilson, and Debrework Zewdie. The input of colleagues in partner agencies—particularly UNAIDS, World Health Organization/Eastern Mediterranean Regional Office, United Nations Children's Fund, and United Nations Office on Drugs and Crime—is much appreciated. Darcy Gallucio provided editorial support and staff of the World Bank External Affairs and Communications in charge of publishing the strategy contributed to the overall quality.

The preparation of this regional strategy was cofinanced by the Global HIV/AIDS Program of the World Bank through the UNAIDS Unified Budget and Workplan Trust Fund and by the MENA Region of the World Bank.

Abbreviations and Acronyms

AIDS	Acquired Immunodeficiency Syndrome
ART	Antiretroviral therapy
CAS	Country Assistance Strategy
CBO	Community-based organization
CEDPA	Center for Development and Population Activities
CSW	Commercial sex worker
EMRO	Eastern Mediterranean Regional Office, WHO
ESW/AAA	Economic and Sector Work/Analytical and Advisory Activities
FHI	Family Health International
FSW	Female sex worker
GAMET	Global HIV/AIDS Monitoring and Evaluation Team
GDP	Gross domestic product
GFATM	Global Fund to Fight AIDS, Tuberculosis and Malaria
GTZ	Deutsche Gesellschaft für Technische Zusammenarbeit
HAART	Highly active antiretroviral therapy
HIV	Human Immunodeficiency Virus
HNP	Health, nutrition, and population
IDA	International Development Association
IDF	Institutional Development Fund
IDP	Internally displaced persons
IDU	Injecting drug user
IEC	Information, education, and communication
ILO	International Labour Organization
IPPF	International Planned Parenthood Federation
KAP	Knowledge, attitude, practice
M&E	Monitoring and evaluation
MDG	Millennium Development Goals
MENA	Middle East and North Africa
MNSHD	Human Development Sector of MENA Region
MoH	Ministry of Health

MSM	Men who have sex with men (or males who have sex with males)
MTCT	Mother-to-child transmission
NAP	National AIDS Program
NAMRU-3	U.S. Naval Medical Research Unit-3
NGO	Nongovernmental organization
NSP	National Strategic Plan
OPEC	Organization of the Petroleum Exporting Countries
PAF	Program Acceleration Funds
PER	Public Expenditure Review
PLWHAs	People living with HIV/AIDS
PMSP	Persons with multiple sex partners
PRSPs	Poverty Reduction Strategy Papers
STD/STI	Sexually transmitted disease/infection
TB	Tuberculosis
UNAIDS	Joint United Nations Programme on HIV/AIDS
UNDP	United Nations Development Programme
UNESCO	United Nations Educational, Scientific, and Cultural Organization
UNFPA	United Nations Population Fund
UNICEF	United Nations Children's Fund
UNODC	United Nations Office on Drugs and Crime
UNODCCP	United Nations Office for Drug Control and Crime Prevention
USAID	United States Agency for International Development
VCT	Voluntary counseling and testing
WBI	World Bank Institute
WHO	World Health Organization

Executive Summary

Introduction

This document presents the rationale for addressing HIV/AIDS in the Middle East and North Africa (MENA) region (including Algeria, Bahrain, Djibouti, the Arab Republic of Egypt, the Islamic Republic of Iran, Iraq, Israel, Jordan, Kuwait, Lebanon, Libya, Morocco, Oman, Qatar, Saudi Arabia, the Syrian Arab Republic, Tunisia, the United Arab Emirates, the West Bank and Gaza, and the Republic of Yemen)[1] and the Bank's strategic choices in supporting countries to prevent the spread of the disease. These choices are based on the Bank's comparative advantage as a knowledge-based financial institution. The World Bank considers meeting the Millennium Development Goals (MDGs) a corporate priority and, in fact, the MDGs provide the global framework on which the MENA regional strategy is based. Two interrelated MDGs are to (1) eradicate extreme poverty and hunger and (2) halt and begin to reverse the spread of HIV/AIDS by 2015. Studies have shown that poverty and income inequality facilitate the diffusion of HIV epidemics and that HIV prevalence levels increase when income per capita declines and inequality increases. While abject poverty in the region remains low, a significant proportion (23.2 percent) of the population lives on less than $2 per day (all dollar amounts are U.S. dollars unless otherwise indicated) and are extremely vulnerable in their ability to cope with shocks. HIV/AIDS is one of the shocks that can drive vulnerable households into abject poverty, a situation which the Bank is working to prevent. The HIV/AIDS epidemic has the potential to impede and even reverse development if not addressed early enough. To preserve the benefits of national and regional development investments put in place by governments and development partners including the World Bank, greater investments to improve HIV/AIDS advocacy, information base, and prevention strategies are needed to maintain low prevalence levels.

The World Health Organization (WHO) and Joint United Nations Programme on HIV/AIDS (UNAIDS) estimates for 2003 (considered to be conservative) indicate a total of 97,000–100,000 people living with HIV in the MENA region today. Most MENA countries are still at an early stage of the HIV infection with a 0.3 percent regional prevalence. What makes the HIV/AIDS epidemic particularly lethal is that it remains invisible for a long period of time and has an incubation period of five to eight years, separating HIV infection from the AIDS stage. As has happened in other countries, if action to prevent this is not taken early, MENA countries face the risk that the HIV infection will spread through the general population. The option of waiting to act until the HIV prevalence rate rises further in the general population would be a costly one. By that time, a general epidemic would be well on its way and, as shown by the international evidence, it would then be too late to prevent the inevitable increase in human sufferings as well as associated losses in economic growth.

Regional HIV/AIDS Risk Factors

Although the weak HIV/AIDS surveillance system in the MENA region indicates a low prevalence scenario, risk factors for the spread of the infection exist in the region. The four key interrelated risk factors present in most of the countries of the region are (1) behavioral risks such as injecting drug use (IDU), commercial sex work (CSW), men who have sex with men (MSM), persons with multiple sex partners, unprotected sexual activities; (2) rising youth population who are particularly at high risk of infection; (3) sexually transmitted infections and low condom use; and (4) structural factors (such as poverty, unemployment of youth, labor migration, gender inequality, gender-based violence, discrimination, and so on), conflict, and refugees. While the epidemic in the region is currently limited to high-risk groups, these are not an isolated group and their interactions with the general populace put the whole region at risk. Interrupting the transmission of the infection to the general populace is crucial and needs to be done in a timely manner. As prevalence rates rise, the impact on human cost begins to shift from being limited to a personal-level issue of the pain and guilt surrounding intimate relationships to a state-level issue threatening economic, social, and political securities.

Framework of Strategic Interventions: Advocacy, Information/Knowledge, and Prevention

For low HIV/AIDS prevalence settings such as the MENA region, countries must be prepared to act primarily at three key levels of interventions:

advocacy, information/knowledge, and prevention in order to keep prevalence rates low. These three interventions must be implemented concurrently to be effective in keeping prevalence rates low. An enabling environment within which these interventions can take place is essential. Advocacy to raise the awareness of leaders regarding the issues, and reduce the stigmas associated with the disease is key to achieving this. Within an enabling environment, people at risk can be empowered to take greater control of their own lives and safety as it concerns the infection. Empowering people will require governments to reduce barriers (such as policies, regulations, customs, and attitudes) at all levels that the populace face, which prevent them from adequately protecting themselves. Combining knowledge with reduced barriers and services will facilitate empowerment of individuals and communities in a way that enables them to alter risky practices and access needed services, leading to a reduction in transmission of HIV. Implementing effective prevention programs that incorporate these elements will require knowledge of the major factors that influence risk taking among people whose lifestyles will likely expose themselves and others to HIV. The figure below shows the conceptual framework to keep prevalence rates low in the MENA region.

In 2003, a global HIV prevention working group estimated that the region requires a tenfold increase in current spending to mount the kind of prevention response capable of preventing a significant outbreak of

FIGURE 1

Conceptual Framework for Preventing HIV/AIDS in Low Prevalence Settings*

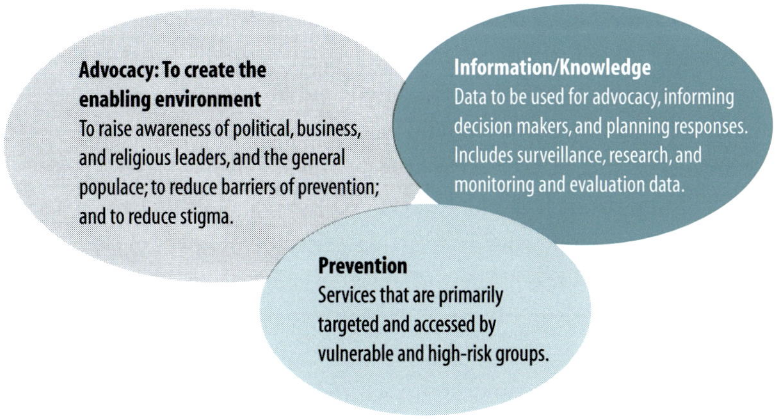

Source: Author's creation.

* While this framework advocates keeping HIV prevalence rates low, the strategy also acknowledges that care and treatment services also need to be provided to those who are already infected and need antiretroviral therapy.

HIV/AIDS. Beyond these financial needs, however, MENA countries need to be prepared to mount the effective actions against HIV/AIDS described above, which experience from other regions has shown could take years to develop. While the infection is still largely confined to vulnerable groups, countries with low prevalence epidemics must be ready to take advantage of the opportunity to create an enabling environment and improve their information/knowledge base to implement prevention efforts among these groups. This approach would be more effective and less costly than having to deal with a full-blown epidemic.

Popular, political, business, and religious leaders must be solicited to help create the enabling environment within which effective prevention activities can be conducted. Usually, legislative change is also required, and legal reform takes time. The MENA region is lagging on most fronts in its defense against HIV. Most decision makers in the region have not considered investment in HIV prevention a high priority. HIV/AIDS is a developmental issue that requires collaborative and multisectoral efforts of many partners beyond the health sector. Coordinating these efforts will require political commitment at the highest levels. The challenge will be to implement HIV/AIDS programs in a more integrated approach rather than as vertical programs. Currently, the range of responses to the HIV/AIDS threat in the region is wide; however, to date no country has implemented an integrated, multisectoral, national program.

The MENA region is characterized by a profound lack of data on the nature and dynamics of its HIV epidemics to use for advocacy, informing decision makers, and planning responses. While national HIV surveillance focuses on relatively low-risk groups, the virus can spread to the general population from high-risk groups. In the absence of adequate surveillance systems, as is the case in most MENA countries, there are no early warning systems that would alert public health officials to detect outbreaks among high-risk populations. Such a situation allows the HIV infection to spread to the general population, at which point it becomes more difficult and expensive to control the HIV/AIDS epidemic. The end result is to transform a public health issue into a disease that affects the economic and social course of countries for many decades to come.

In addition to the lack of hard data, high levels of stigma and discrimination against people with HIV/AIDS exist in almost all of the MENA countries (as elsewhere in the world). The silence surrounding sexual issues limits the opportunities to introduce sexual education in schools and set up prevention measures. The stigma also drives people living with HIV/AIDS (PLWHAs) and high-risk groups underground, which further complicates the task of epidemiological surveillance. The stigma is made worse by the broad lack of understanding of HIV/AIDS, which translates into a lack of protective behavior. The stigma of HIV/AIDS leads to many serious problems as countries attempt to respond to the epidemic. For example, use of voluntary counseling and testing (VCT) services is hampered by high levels of HIV-related stigma, as is the access to antiretroviral therapy (ART).

Why Act Now?

As is currently evident in other regions, even in low prevalence countries, the situation can change rapidly for the worse if action is not taken early enough. Despite the conservative estimates of HIV infections in the MENA region, research has shown that future losses of potential output and consumption over the next 25 years because of the epidemic could be in the order of 35 percent of current gross domestic product (GDP). While the epidemic situation in the region may never reach the proportions that exist in Sub-Saharan Africa today, the HIV prevalence rates and risk factors in the MENA region indicate that HIV/AIDS will be a continued burden on the economies of the region. Collective research and evidence has shown the economic and social benefits of tackling HIV/AIDS epidemics while prevalence rates are low. International experience has also shown that low-cost prevention strategies are efficient in slowing the spread of HIV/AIDS and that the costs of these actions are more than compensated by the savings they generate. Additionally, the Copenhagen Consensus 2004 expert panel of world leading economists has recommended that combating HIV/AIDS prevention be placed at the top of the world's priority list based on an analysis of the costs and benefits of 10 top global challenges. There is no doubt that the MENA region is currently facing a variety of security and development-related crises, but this state of affairs is leading to a lack of attention to the insidious entry of HIV/AIDS into the region. With other far more visible health problems and high levels of stigma associated with HIV/AIDS, few people see the suffering of those with HIV/AIDS. MENA countries have a unique window of opportunity to stem the tide of HIV/AIDS while prevalence rates are still low and when early interventions can bring higher benefits at lower costs.

In principle, allocating public funds for an epidemic such as HIV involves a decision process quite similar to other decisions about the use of public funds. It entails comparing today's cost of implementing a program of HIV/AIDS activities with the enhanced economic and social development made possible by the subsequent reduction in the prevalence of HIV/AIDS. In the case of MENA countries, the choice they face is quite straightforward: either pay a small cost now to implement intervention measures or defer action and incur a much higher cost later on. Because the epidemic is still at an early stage, the intervention measures would consist mainly of advocacy for political action, improved surveillance activities (to remedy the shortcomings of the current system and provide information for better planning), prevention activities targeting specific groups, and information and education campaigns (IEC) for the general population. Achieving the HIV/AIDS goal (and other goals) of the MDGs, requires evidenced-based and focused policies that can be put in place only when adequate data on the epidemic are available.

Justification for World Bank Action

This strategy has been developed to meet the imperative for investing early in this epidemic, and the following justify the Bank's involvement in HIV/AIDS programming in the region:

- Investing now makes economic and social sense. As an example, economic analysis shows that expanding access to safe needles for IDUs and increasing condom use in the region can generate savings equivalent to 20 percent of today's GDP.
- Investing in HIV/AIDS programming is consistent with the Bank's overall poverty and reduction strategy and corporate priorities and, therefore, is a corporate responsibility.
- Investing in HIV/AIDS programming supports the two pillars of the region's corporate strategy (improving the investment climate and empowering poor people to participate in development) as well as the regional social development strategy.
- There is a window of opportunity now to be proactive rather than reactive to the growing epidemic.
- There is growing interest among client countries to address HIV/AIDS.
- With the multisectoral effects of HIV/AIDS, investments made by the Bank to address the epidemic now will have a multiplying effect beyond the health sector to many other development sectors.

Objective and Priorities

The objective of this regional strategy is to clarify the role of the Bank in confronting the HIV/AIDS epidemic in the region based on a review of regional and country needs and gaps, regional and national responses to the needs, and the areas in which the Bank is best positioned to support countries' efforts. Having reviewed the available evidence and held consultative meetings with other stakeholders, the following four priority areas have been identified, which fit into the conceptual framework that integrates advocacy, information, and prevention interventions.

1. **Engage political leaders, policy makers, and key stakeholders to raise awareness and increase the priority given to HIV/AIDS programs within national and regional development agendas.** Bank support (through policy dialogue with clients during preparation of country assistance strategy [CAS], public expenditure review [PER], poverty reduction strategy papers [PRSPs], and the convening of conferences/meetings) would contribute to advocacy efforts and concurrently to creating an enabling environment within which countries can increase their knowledge base and provide targeted prevention services.

2. **Support the upgrading of the surveillance systems and strengthen research and evaluation of epidemiological, economic, and behavioral aspects of HIV/AIDS to enhance the effectiveness of HIV/AIDS policies and programs.** While directly supporting the information/knowledge base of the region, Bank intervention in this area (through Economic and Sector Work/Analytical and Advisory Activities [ESW/AAA], monitoring and evaluation [M&E], research, and so on) would concurrently provide the data needed for more effective advocacy and the planning and design of targeted prevention, care and treatment services.

3. **Support the development of national HIV/AIDS strategies and programs, based on the specific epidemiological, social, and economic conditions and context of each country.** Bank support (through technical assistance, fostering multisectoral and regional collaboration, integration of HIV/AIDS into multisectoral projects, and so on) would concurrently contribute to the three levels of intervention of the conceptual framework.

4. **Support capacity building and knowledge sharing for the comprehensive management of HIV/AIDS programs.** Bank intervention (through technical assistance, capacity building in collaboration with World Bank Institute [WBI] and the Bank's Global HIV/AIDS Unit, Global HIV/AIDS Monitoring and Evaluation Team [GAMET], ACTAfrica, and so on) would primarily support the knowledge base and prevention services but also would contribute to creating an enabling environment.

Based on the Bank's comparative advantage of being a financial institution, skilled in economic and social analysis, and a convener of stakeholders and resources, the role of the Bank in the four areas of intervention will vary from leadership to active partnership and participation. The Bank will collaborate with other developmental agencies in the region and beyond to help governments work in a comprehensive and harmonized manner.

Timeline and Criteria for Intervention

Some activities, like engaging political leaders and strengthening the knowledge base, which can be easily integrated into ongoing bank business, can take place in the short to medium term without much of an incremental budget. But others, such as promoting multisectoral policy and response and capacity building, will require additional resources and have to be planned in the medium to long term. The criteria for the Bank's involvement in HIV/AIDS programming in a country include the following: (1) ongoing dialogue between the Bank and the country and, as an extension, in cases in which policy dialogue tools like CASs and PERs are under preparation; (2) evidence of the government's commitment to address HIV/AIDS (such as the existence of a national HIV/AIDS strategic plan and dedicated resources) and expressed interest by the country for the Bank to support its efforts; (3) opportunity to work with other development partners (for example, the UN Theme Groups on HIV/AIDS) and leverage technical and financial resources (for example, existence of resources from the Global Fund to Fight HIV/AIDS, Tuberculosis and Malaria; the Ford Foundation; and the United States Agency for International Development [USAID]); (4) ongoing Bank projects/interventions in which HIV/AIDS activities can be retrofitted; and (5) presence of an enabling environment for the Bank to work in an intersectoral manner.

Using these criteria, this strategy has identified a number of countries where the available but limited resources can immediately be put to best use. These countries include Djibouti,[2] the Islamic Republic of Iran, Jordan, Lebanon, Morocco, and the Republic of Yemen. Other countries can be added to this list as resources become available and interest in the Bank's assistance increases. There is insufficient information on the epidemic in the Gulf countries to make a case for immediate interventions beyond continuing advocacy for action. Within the countries where the Bank intervenes, the priority groups that have been identified for focused interventions are IDUs, CSWs, prisoners, the youth, and MSM.

Resource Implications

Implementing this strategy in the short to medium term will require resources for ESW/AAA tasks to increase the knowledge base, incorporating HIV/AIDS programming into CASs and other policy dialogue tools,
retrofitting HIV/AIDS activities into projects in which governments are
so willing, consultative meetings with regional partners and stakeholders,
awareness raising and capacity building for Bank and regional staff, and
the Bank staff time needed to implement these activities. The need for innovative financing mechanisms is key, because the region is mainly composed of middle-income countries where financing through lending oper-
ations on HIV/AIDS will be less significant than in low-income countries,
particularly if governments can access grants from other sources.

Notes

1. These countries comprise the World Bank's MENA regional definition, which
   is not synonymous with that of other UN agencies. The UNAIDS region
   includes the Sudan and Somalia but omits Israel. The EMRO/WHO region
   includes the Sudan, Somalia, Pakistan, and Afghanistan but omits Algeria and
   Israel.
2. Assistance to Djibouti will likely vary from other countries, because it is
   already relatively well funded with a stand-alone HIV/AIDS project. Therefore, Bank assistance will more likely focus on synergizing the experience of
   Djibouti with other countries of the region.

Introduction

While it is acknowledged that HIV/AIDS is only one of many serious threats facing the Middle East and North Africa (MENA) region, the World Bank has a corporate agenda for controlling HIV/AIDS. Experience from other regions of the world with more advanced epidemics clearly indicates how devastating it is to ignore the need for investments to prevent the spread of HIV/AIDS while prevalence rates are low. It is precisely this context of low HIV/AIDS prevalence in the region that provides a unique window of opportunity today to control and avert a catastrophic epidemic in the future. Countries of the region need to be supported in adequately preparing themselves to address the impact of the epidemic.

The objective of this regional strategy is to clarify the role of the Bank in confronting the HIV/AIDS epidemic in the region based on a review of regional and country needs and gaps, as well as the areas in which the Bank is best positioned to support countries' efforts. To fully achieve this objective, the strategy also reviews and assesses the degree to which responses by governments, nongovernmental organizations (NGOs), and bilateral and multilateral partners have met national needs. This strategy has attempted to identify appropriate instruments for implementing the Bank's support agenda. Based on the paucity of data and the early stage of the epidemic, this strategy provides guidance more at an aggregate/regional level than on a country-by-country basis, which requires more in-depth and country-specific analyses that are best coordinated by the countries themselves.

This document has identified four key strategic directions based on the abovementioned regional and country reviews as well as on the Bank's comparative advantages. The order of priority may vary for each country, depending on specific situations and the presence of support from other development partners. The role of the Bank within each strategic direction will also vary based on the specific sets of skills that are most needed. Because of the evolving nature of the epidemic and the lack of adequate surveillance data in the region, this strategy is not intended to be a static document but one that will continue to evolve to respond to new and updated data to ensure that it remains responsive to the actual needs of the region.

This strategic document provides guidance on focal issues for discussion by the Bank with governments and development partners of the region. In this regard, the three main audiences of the strategy will be MENA Region Bank staff, client country governments, and regional development partners. For the Bank staff, the strategy is both an advocacy tool on the importance of incorporating HIV/AIDS components in their ongoing and planned activities and a tool that provides guidance on strategies to achieve these goals. For governments and development partners, the strategy is an advocacy tool and one that highlights possible areas of support and collaboration to reduce the spread and impact of the epidemic in the region.

Chapter 1 presents the situational analysis, the justification for World Bank action, and the epidemiological context of the epidemic in the region. Chapter 2 describes the responses from countries, UN agencies, bilateral donors, NGOs, and the private sector, and identifies challenges and gaps in relation to the priority needs by country and across the region. Chapter 3 identifies the four proposed key strategic directions based on information from the previous two chapters. The chapter concludes with a brief review of anticipated risks and challenges associated with implementing the strategy.

CHAPTER 1

Situational Analysis, Justification, and Epidemiological Context

Situational Analysis: The Silent Threat Grows

The MENA region is currently facing a variety of security and development-related crises. While the range of disturbances is great—from the conflict and occupation in Iraq and the West Bank and Gaza to more subtle political uneasiness in several other countries—HIV/AIDS is only one of many serious threats and not yet a particularly visible one. The recent history of the HIV pandemic, however, clearly shows how devastating it is to ignore the need for investments to prevent the spread of HIV while prevalence is still low. This is particularly true given the degree of instability, economic stagnation, and conflict in the region.

Throughout the world, the HIV epidemic has shown that those who have the least agency to control their own lives are the most at risk of infection. These are generally the poor, the marginalized, the young, and women. In the MENA region, as in many others, these at-risk populations also include migrants in search of work, internally displaced persons (IDPs), and refugees. Although the estimates made by some MENA region officials and the Joint United Nations Programme on HIV/AIDS/World Health Organization (UNAIDS/WHO) are based on inadequate data,[1] estimates published for 2003 stated that there were between 43,000 and 67,000 new HIV cases among children and adults in the region (as defined by UNAIDS/WHO). Even without knowing whether this represents an increase over the previous years, it is clear that unless there is swift action there can only be future increases. The MENA region is poised for a potential epidemic that can be averted through the application of evidence-based strategies, successful prevention methods, and adequate care and treatment for those who are already infected. While the last few years have seen substantial progress in developing a response in several countries in the region, most countries still lack both high-level political commitment and grassroots capacity. There is a real danger that in the MENA region, as in countries with more advanced epidemics, people will have to experience the frequent deaths of family members, friends, and neighbors before they respond with a sense of urgency. Complacency is one of HIV's greatest allies.

Many of the factors that place people at risk of acquiring an HIV infection are beyond their own control, such as labor policies, women's legal and social rights, and poor health systems. These issues must be examined and managed at a structural level. The choices are to act now to prevent a probable epidemic or to remain complacent and face a probable crisis in the near future. MENA countries have a unique window of opportunity to stem the tide of HIV/AIDS while the prevalence rates are still low.

HIV/AIDS cannot be considered a simple medical problem that can be managed with a typical public health approach. Health services alone cannot produce the breadth of responses necessary to reduce vulnerability. A coordinated multisectoral response is needed that includes appropriate government departments, UN agencies, multilateral and bilateral donors, the private sector, NGOs, and community-based groups.

There will be no better opportunity in the future to avert thousands of HIV infections than there is today.

Justification for World Bank Action

HIV/AIDS is only one of many serious threats facing the Middle East and North Africa region. The World Bank has a corporate agenda for controlling HIV/AIDS, as global experience has shown how devastating it is to miss the opportunity to prevent the spread of HIV/AIDS while prevalence rates are low. From the very limited data that are available, it is clear that HIV/AIDS prevalence rates in the MENA region are low, but there are also indications that that infection rates could increase rapidly based on the existence of key risk factors for the infection. Countries in MENA have a clear but limited window for action within which to effectively control and avert a looming epidemic in the future. Following are several important reasons for investing early to prevent further spreading of this epidemic:

1. Investing now makes economic and social sense. Keeping prevalence levels low will reduce not only the human cost of the epidemic but also the social, economic, and political costs that would have major impacts on the future economies of countries and on the region as a whole. Even with the current low HIV prevalence in the MENA region, economic analysis has demonstrated that future losses of potential output and consumption over the next 25 years because of the epidemic could

be in the order of 35 percent of current gross domestic product (GDP). Studies have shown that while prevalence levels are low, investments made to avert further infections will also be low compared with investments made when prevalence rates are higher. As an example, economic analysis indicates that expanding access to safe needles for injecting drug users (IDUs) and increasing condom use in the region can generate savings equivalent to 20 percent of today's GDP. Annex 1 provides a detailed economic analysis of the epidemic in the region.

As prevalence rates rise, the impact on health status, health expenditures, and labor productivity because of loss of human capital, as well as reductions in life expectancy and other socioeconomic consequences, become increasingly greater, forcing governments to make important budgetary reallocations. These budgetary reallocations from more productive economic activities like education and rural development, can lead to reductions in aggregate economic efficiency and put additional pressures on long-term economic growth. Inaction while prevalence rates are low is not a viable economic option for the Bank nor for countries of the region.

2. Investing in HIV/AIDS programming is consistent with the Bank's overall poverty reduction strategy and corporate agenda. Because HIV/AIDS has been shown to cause and worsen poverty,[2] any poverty reduction strategy that omits investment in HIV/AIDS control cannot be considered a comprehensive strategy in a region where obvious risk factors for rising HIV infections exist. In the long run, inaction on the HIV/AIDS front has been shown to undermine development efforts and actually reverse previous gains. Economic analyses of the impact of the epidemic have shown that, depending on how sensitive poverty prevalence is to economic growth, the number of people in the MENA region who would have failed to escape poverty by 2010 because of HIV/AIDS could range from 8 million to 30 million. By investing in HIV/AIDS programming in the MENA region, the Bank will be supporting these countries to preserve their development achievements and prospects.

Included in the Bank's corporate agenda is the acceleration of programming toward achieving the Millennium Development Goals (MDGs), one of which is to halt and begin to reverse the spread of HIV/AIDS by 2015. HIV/AIDS control is a corporate priority on the basis of the MDGs and the epidemic's potential to impede or even reverse development gains. As with the other MDGs, HIV/AIDS has cross-sectoral determinants that will require intersectoral action and synergies in analytics, policy, and programming, areas in which the Bank is competent.

3. Investing in HIV/AIDS programming supports the two pillars of the region's corporate strategy—improving the investment climate for investment, jobs, and sustainable growth, and empowering poor people to participate in development and investing in them—as well as the regional social development strategy. While poverty levels are relatively low in the region, the proportion of the affected populations in the MENA region is still significant as is the proportion of the populations that are vulnerable to lapsing into poverty.[3] Investing in HIV/AIDS programming can address a critical factor that could drive many vulnerable MENA households into poverty. The region also faces the second highest unemployment rates in the world, making it critical to create employment opportunities for young adults who, because of their age and social circumstances, also happen to be most susceptible to acquiring HIV. Investing in HIV/AIDS programming while prevalence levels are low is an effective way of ensuring sustainable growth in the region.

   Addressing HIV/AIDS in the region supports the social development strategy of the region that, among other goals, aims to promote the inclusion of the poor, vulnerable, and excluded groups, especially women and youth.[4] The social strategy also aims to strengthen social cohesion and people's capacity for collective development actions. These are the same social dynamics of inclusion that are absolutely necessary for sustainable management and control of HIV/AIDS.

4. There is a window of opportunity now to be proactive. While the low HIV/AIDS prevalence in MENA does not equate to low risk, it does provide a unique window of opportunity for the Bank and client countries in the region to prevent the further spread of the epidemic. The region needs to be more proactive than reactive to the epidemic, while there is time to keep prevalence rates low and contain the epidemic. The next few years are critical and offer an opportunity to take advantage of successful examples from other regions for the design of HIV/AIDS prevention programs. However, the opportunity has to be taken now to benefit from this advantage.

5. There is growing interest among client countries to address HIV/AIDS. Fourteen out of 19 countries of the region have UN Theme Groups devoted to HIV/AIDS, and at least two countries have requested the Bank's involvement in Theme Group activities. Seven countries have or are in the process of developing their national HIV/AIDS strategic plans. Six countries have requested and received approval for funding of HIV/AIDS activities from the Global Fund to Fight HIV/AIDS, Tuberculosis, and Malaria (GFATM).

6. Investments made toward controlling the spread of HIV/AIDS will have multiplying effects in all development sectors. Any investments the Bank makes to support capacity building in the area of HIV/AIDS surveillance and behavioral research, for example, will have positive effects on the surveillance of other health conditions. Investments in effective HIV/AIDS health services will benefit the treatment of other sexually transmitted infections (STIs) and blood-borne viruses (for example, hepatitis C in the Islamic Republic of Iran) that are managed in similar ways. The same goes for investments in other sectors in which, for example, any progress made in better understanding the determinants of poverty and risk behaviors as they relate to HIV/AIDS in the region is likely to benefit the activities in several sectors. Investing across sectors will also provide an opportunity to promote multisectoral planning and partnership not only on HIV/AIDS but also on other issues that require intersectoral action.

Current Knowledge of the Epidemic in the Region

The region is characterized by a profound lack of accurate and useful information on the nature and dynamics of its HIV epidemics. A recent Bank report on HIV/AIDS in the region concludes that, "In sum, the most important information needed to plan and design HIV/sexually transmitted disease (STD) prevention programs in the region is lacking" (Jenkins and Robalino 2003). This remains true, despite a few recent attempts to improve the information base. Recent evidence suggests that the incidence of STIs is increasing and the total number of AIDS deaths has increased almost sixfold since the early 1990s. There is little clarity, however, in most countries regarding either incidence (new infections) or prevalence (accumulated percentage) of HIV infections. Recent evidence suggests that the number of adults and children living with HIV/AIDS is rising rapidly in MENA countries (see figure 1.1).

The serious lack of adequate surveillance and standardized reporting precludes the construction of an accurate regional epidemiological profile. To date, information systems are usually based on detection through mandatory testing in low-risk general population groups, such as blood donors or tuberculosis (TB) patients,[5] and occasional surveys of presumed at-risk groups in detention or prisons, with an ill-defined sampling that is inadequate for establishing trends. This type of surveillance is not recommended for low prevalence countries, where it is essential to monitor prevalence among those most at risk of becoming infected. Standardization of reporting across the region has yet to be achieved, making estimation of prevalence levels almost impossible. Furthermore, information

FIGURE 1.1

Percentage Increase in the Numbers of Adults and Children Living with HIV/AIDS, 2001–03

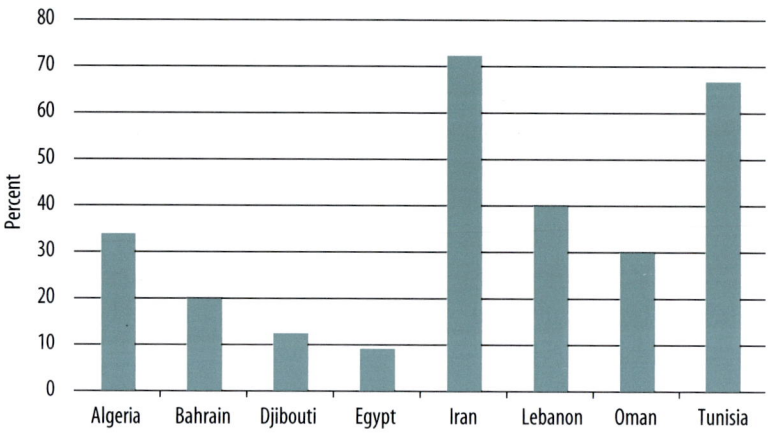

Source: UNAIDS/WHO 2003.

is commonly not shared or made available to legitimate HIV/AIDS implementation partners.

The reported AIDS statistics for 1990 to mid-2003 are given in Annex 2, while Annex 3 presents the profiles of the epidemic for countries of the region. Reported AIDS cases (representing cases of advanced symptomatic AIDS-related diseases entering the public hospital systems) do not indicate the extent of HIV prevalence, its trends, or the directions in which the various epidemics are moving. Unlinked anonymous surveillance systems that could indicate early trends have not yet been developed. It is doubtful that the capacity currently exists in many of the region's countries to reach out to the most at-risk groups for testing and surveillance, both serological and behavioral. Political sensitivity may continue to hamper collecting information on these particular groups. Whatever the reasons are, proper second-generation surveillance, including the monitoring of HIV, risk behaviors, and STIs, is an essential missing element for HIV/AIDS control.

Coupled with the lack of hard data to use for advocacy, informing decision makers and planning responses, and high levels of stigma and discrimination against people with HIV/AIDS exist in almost all of the MENA countries as elsewhere in the world. This delays the development of adequate epidemiological surveillance as well as interventions. When the principal information people receive about the disease casts it only as an infection of IDUs, men who have sex with men (MSM), and those who practice illicit sex, no one wants to be associated with it in any way. Efforts must be made to engage religious and other social leaders in a dialogue that will help them understand how they can diminish such attitudes and preconceptions among the people they influence.

The stigma of HIV/AIDS leads to many serious problems as countries attempt to respond to the epidemic. For example, use of voluntary counseling and testing (VCT) services is hampered by high levels of HIV-related stigma, as is the access to antiretroviral therapy (ART). In much of the region, confidentiality is not guaranteed, except perhaps with private providers. It can be assumed that most people seek private medical care if they suspect they have HIV. Private health facilities, which provide the bulk of diagnosis and treatment in the region, are unregulated and are not required to report results of HIV testing to government health agencies. Therefore, current methods of detection produce considerable levels of underreporting and promote the false impression that the epidemic is not a growing problem. Addressing the dual problem of general population education and the reduction of stigma is a fundamental intervention aimed at reducing widespread barriers to improved prevention and care.

Table 1.1 lists the UNAIDS/WHO estimates of the number of people living with HIV/AIDS by country between 2001 and 2003. Nevertheless, based on these estimates, by the end of 2003 there were approximately 111,500 persons living with HIV/AIDS in the MENA region as defined by the World Bank. While these regional figures are relatively low, low prevalence does not equate to low risks and should not mean low priority. Inadequate surveillance methods can overlook outbreaks in marginalized social groups. Furthermore, even in low prevalence nations, the situation can change rapidly for the worse, as has occurred in Indonesia, Nepal, Vietnam, and China.

The estimated 111,500 persons living with HIV/AIDS in the region are people who now require monitoring, care, support, and eventually treatment. These people and their families need services that could mitigate the impact of HIV on their lives, including the spread of HIV to others. With the increasing proportion of females becoming infected in several countries (Algeria, Morocco, Oman, and the Republic of Yemen), the coming years will require increased investment in screening antenatal women and offering the means to prevent vertical transmission from mother to child through childbirth and breastfeeding.

These 111,500 people are, however, people who have already been infected within the past 5 to 10 years. More importantly, from a public health point of view, these estimates offer no indication as to who is at greatest risk of acquiring the virus today and, therefore, where targeted prevention activities must be focused now. Without behavioral surveillance of the most vulnerable populations, such information is lacking.

TABLE 1.1

Estimated Number of People Living with HIV/AIDS in MENA Countries

Country	Number of Adults and Children Living with HIV		Prevalence Rate (% population)		Increase between 2001 and 2003
	2001	2003	2001	2003	%
Algeria	6,800	9,100	0.02%	0.03%	33.8%
Bahrain	<500	600	<0.08%	0.09%	20.0%
Djibouti	8,100	9,100	1.26%	1.41%	12.3%
Egypt, Arab Rep. of	11,000	12,000	0.02%	0.02%	9.1%
Iran, Islamic Rep. of	18,000	31,000	0.03%	0.04%	72.2%
Iraq	–	500	–	0.00%	–
Israel	–	3,000	–	0.05%	–
Jordan	600	600	0.01%	0.01%	0.0%
Kuwait	–	–	–	–	–
Lebanon	2,000	2,800	0.11%	0.15%	40.0%
Libya	–	10,000	–	0.18%	–
Morocco	–	15,000	–	0.05%	–
Oman	1,000	1,300	0.04%	0.05%	30.0%
Qatar	–	<1000	–	<0.17%	–
Saudi Arabia	–	–	–	–	–
Syrian Arab Rep.	–	<500	–	<0.003%	–
Tunisia	600	1000	0.006%	0.010%	66.7%
United Arab Emirates	–	<1000	–	<0.04%	–
West Bank and Gaza	–	<1000	–	<0.03%	–
Yemen, Republic of	–	12,000	–	0.06%	–

Source: Based on data from "2004 Report on the Global AIDS Epidemic" (UNAIDS 2004).
–: not available

Systematic estimations of the size of at-risk groups have not been at-tempted, which is a necessary step in the further development of estimates listed in Table 1.1 and the formulation of intervention programs. The predictable costs of care are doubtlessly already rising (usually at least half of these costs are borne directly by individuals and families in the private sector), while investment in much-needed targeted interventions for high-risk groups have not even begun in the majority of countries.

Risk Factors in the Region

The following section summarizes four key interrelated risk factors for HIV/AIDS in the region.

1. Behavioral Risks

- IDUs—The use of injecting drugs has been noted in Bahrain, Egypt, the Islamic Republic of Iran, Israel, Lebanon, Libya, Morocco, Oman, Saudi Arabia, Tunisia, and the West Bank and Gaza (in the general and the incarcerated populations). Indirectly related to this is the widespread illicit use of non-injecting drugs among males, which can lead to IDU or disinhibit users, impairing judgment and thus leading to sexual risk taking.

- Commercial sex workers (CSW)—This includes the widespread sex trade, both male and female, urban and rural, registered and clandestine; trafficking and importation of women for sex trade in some countries. CSW clients within and beyond the region include married and unmarried men, traveling businessmen, migrant workers, and unmarried youth.

- MSM—The presence of male-to-male sex has been reported in the region.

- Persons with multiple sex partners (PMSP)—Having multiple sex partners increases the risk of contracting and spreading HIV/AIDS.

2. Rising Youth Population

- The proportion of young people, especially young men, having sex before marriage is significant. The youth population is more vulnerable to engaging in risky activities (for example, unprotected sexual intercourse, injected drug use, and so on).

3. STI and Low Condom Use

- Increasing prevalence of standard STIs in some countries and inadequate knowledge of STIs and modes of prevention. This is coupled with low levels of condom use.

4. Structural Factors, Conflict, and Refugees

- Multiple structural factors contributing to overall vulnerability such as poverty, unemployment of youth, gender-based violence and discrimination, policies relating to refugees and IDPs, inadequate health services, educational policies, labor policies, and so on.

- The high levels of stigma associated with STIs and HIV/AIDS deter infected persons from accessing prevention and care services.

- Conflict situations with the attending political and social changes create a conducive environment for the spread of HIV/AIDS and related to this is the presence of refugees, IDPs, and migrants.

Key Messages and Prerequisites for Action

Low HIV/AIDS awareness and increasing risk behaviors can potentially lead to significant HIV transmission in the region. While surveillance in the region is known to be generally weak, available data show notable infection rates among IDUs, CSWs and their clients, and among MSM. The region urgently needs to invest in strengthening its knowledge and database on the epidemic with which it can eventually invest in evidenced-based HIV/AIDS programs. As a prerequisite for action, the Bank and other regional partners will have to engage leaders and decision makers at the local, national, and regional levels in the discourse on HIV/AIDS and support their readiness to address the epidemic while rates are still low. To fully convince stakeholders, the Bank and regional partners will need more reliable data on the epidemic and this can be achieved by supporting the development of second-generation surveillance systems that have been proven to be effective in tracking low prevalence epidemics.

Notes

1. The ranges around the estimates define the boundaries within which the actual numbers lie, based on the best available information. These ranges are more precise than those of previous years and work is under way to increase the precision of the estimates that will be published in mid-2004 (UNAIDS/WHO 2003), but accuracy depends on adequate estimates of the size of risk groups and that information generally is not available in the region.
2. HIV/AIDS can cause and worsen poverty by lost productivity; catastrophic costs of health care; increased dependency ratio; increased number of orphans with poor nutrition; orphan/child-headed households; reduced school enrollment; decreased capacity to manage households; diminished agricultural productivity; reduced national income; and fewer national resources for HIV/AIDS control (World Bank 2001).
3. World Bank 2002.
4. World Bank 2004.
5. TB patients often are surveyed in low prevalence countries because they are accessible and because those in charge of TB programs wish to know what proportion of patients is simultaneously infected with HIV. TB patients cannot, however, be considered as high risk for HIV because the behaviors associated with acquiring HIV are not the same factors for becoming infected with TB.

References

World Bank. 2001. AIDS, Poverty Reduction and Debt Relief: A Toolkit for Mainstreaming HIV/AIDS Programs into Development Instruments. UNAIDS/World Bank Publication, Washington, DC.

———. 2002. Middle East and North Africa Region Strategy Paper. Washington, DC.

———. 2004. Draft. Securing a Future for All: Social Development Strategy for the Middle East and North Africa Region. Washington, DC.

Jenkins, C., and David A. Robalino. 2003. *HIV/AIDS in the Middle East-North Africa: The Costs of Inaction*. Washington, DC: World Bank.

Tawilah, J. 2002. "HIV/AIDS Epidemic in the EMR." PowerPoint presentation, October.

UNAIDS. 2004. "2004 Report on the Global AIDS Epidemic." AIDS Epidemic Update. Geneva: UNAIDS.

UNAIDS/WHO. December 2003. AIDS Epidemic Update. Geneva: UNAIDS.

CHAPTER 2

Responses and Challenges

Most countries in the MENA region began recording cases of AIDS during the latter half of the 1980s and soon thereafter developed national AIDS committees or programs. But, as in so many other regions, the HIV/AIDS epidemic was not viewed as an urgent issue and national responses languished without much accomplishment for years. Few multilateral or bilateral partners provided any financial aid. To date, 14 out of 19 countries in the region have UN Theme Groups devoted to HIV/AIDS.[1] Between 2000 and 2003, however, several countries began to develop real efforts toward prevention, with the Islamic Republic of Iran and Morocco having the most advanced programs.

National Responses

Currently, the range of responses to the HIV/AIDS threat in the region is wide, but no country has implemented an integrated, multisectoral, national program. Heads of State in Djibouti, Libya, the Islamic Republic of Iran, and most recently Algeria have publicly acknowledged the HIV/AIDS problems in their countries. To date, the Islamic Republic of Iran, Lebanon, and Morocco are implementing some programs for at-risk groups, while Algeria and Djibouti are just beginning. Algeria, Egypt, the Islamic Republic of Iran, Lebanon, Morocco, and the Republic of Yemen have developed or are currently developing National Strategic Plans (NSPs), starting with situational assessments and moving to multisectoral strategy development, prioritization, and costing. Bahrain, Jordan, Libya, Oman, Syria, and Tunisia have expressed an interest in doing the same. When NSPs have been developed, technical expertise has not always been adequate and so plans tend to be generic and could be improved in quality and relevance. Table 2.1 provides a snapshot of the different national responses to the epidemic, while Annex 4 provides more details.

TABLE 2.1

National Response to HIV/AIDS Epidemic

Country	National Strategic Plan (NSP)	Status	Next Steps
Algeria	NSP against HIV/AIDS and STIs 2002–06	Operational plans of 10 sectors and 3 NGOs for 2003–06 developed. $6.18 million in support on NSP implementation (GFATM[a]).	Ensuring multisectoral coordination. Implementation of the operational plans.
Djibouti	Multisectoral National Strategic Framework on HIV/AIDS 2003–07	11 sectoral plans developed and costed. $12 million in support of NSP implementation (the World Bank and other partners).	Implementation of the NSP across sectors, including elaboration of operational plans.
Egypt, Arab Rep. of	Assessment of the HIV/AIDS Situation and Response in the Arab Republic of Egypt, 2003	Situation Assessment being validated with national partners.	Development of the NSP.
Iran, Islamic Rep. of	Draft NSP on Prevention and Control of HIV/AIDS 2002–06	Validation at the national level, $9.69 million in support of NSP implementation, including capacity building of NGOs (GFATM[a]).	Development of operational plans of priority sectors, including costing. Implementation of the NSP.
Lebanon	AIDS NSP in Lebanon for 2004–09	NSP has been finalized and is being widely disseminated to diverse partners. Operation plans are being elaborated.	Validation of the operational plans. Initiation of implementation of the NSP and mobilization of resources.
Morocco	NSP 2002–04	Implementation of the NSP initiated through GFATM resources. $4.74 million in support of NSP implementation (GFATM[a]).	Development of the NSP from 2005 onwards and operational sectoral plans, including costing. Scaling up implementation and mobilization of resources.
Yemen, Republic of	National Strategic Framework (NSF) on HIV/AIDS (until 2005)	NSF to be updated.	NSF to be updated.

Source: UNAIDS 2003.

a. GFATM resources are indicated for two-year approved funding.

TABLE 2.2

Countries Approved for GFATM Funding for HIV/AIDS Activities (U.S. Dollars)

Country	Grant Amount	Amount Disbursed	Status
Algeria	$6,185,000	$0	Grant Agreement Signed
Djibouti	7,271,400	0	Board Approved
Iran, Islamic Rep. of (in two grants)	15,396,000	0	Not Yet Signed
Jordan	1,778,600	983,231	Disbursing
Morocco	4,738,806	3,821,919	Disbursing
Yemen, Republic of	5,500,405	0	Board Approved
TOTAL	**40,870,211**	**4,805,150**	

Source: GFATM Web site, accessed October 2004.

While overall, national financial investments on HIV/AIDS have been insufficient in the region, some governments have made serious financial commitments to tackle HIV/AIDS. Recently it has been reported that Libya will allocate $2 million to the HIV/AIDS response in the country, including prevention and care in prisons and treatment centers for IDUs, but the United Nations Office on Drugs and Crime (UNODC) reports that the Libyan program is in great need of technical input. Six countries (Algeria, Djibouti, the Islamic Republic of Iran, Jordan, Morocco, and the Republic of Yemen) have been approved to receive grants for addressing HIV/AIDS from GFATM in the first three funding rounds (see Table 2.2 for details). Of the six MENA countries approved for funding, only two (Jordan and Morocco) have actually received funds so far. Several countries have begun to seek help in building capacity to carry out research, interventions, and monitoring and evaluation (M&E) with the funding they will receive from the GFATM.

As in other countries in the world, over-reliance on medical doctors characterizes the response in several MENA countries. Until the more recent activation of interest among UN cosponsors, only health departments were involved with HIV/AIDS, with support from WHO/Eastern Mediterranean Regional Office (EMRO). Now, however, UN Theme Group chairs are rotated from among all the UN agencies and are not solely from WHO. While this sets the scene for the consideration of a wider multisectoral response, numerous medical issues remain unresolved and need to be addressed in many of the MENA countries. It has been pointed out that, while the medical establishment is pleased to have ART with which to treat HIV disease, there are very few doctors and other health workers who understand how to use ART. Health services in most of the region's countries are not yet prepared to manage the opportunistic infections among many HIV patients. In the poorer countries of the region, health services are generally weak and inadequate and require considerable input in the areas of injection safety, monitoring and screening of blood donations and transfusions, universal precautions, confidentiality, counseling training, and a nondiscriminatory attitude toward HIV/AIDS patients.

Integrating Prevention with Treatment at the National Level

More recently, a number of countries have taken the initiative of offering ART free of charge, despite the cost. In Algeria, the government has made the drugs available free of charge to eligible patients since 1998. By the end of 2003, 100 individuals were under treatment at a cost of $10,000–$15,000 per year for triple therapy, as lower prices have not been negotiated thus far. Similarly, the Lebanese Ministry of Health (MoH) has provided ART free of charge to citizens since 1998 and highly active antiretroviral therapy (HAART) has been available in the private market since 1997. In 2002, 144 individuals were receiving ART at an approximate cost of $1,000/person/month. In Morocco, the government has provided ART to all eligible Moroccan citizens since 1999. By the end of 2003, there were 523 individuals under treatment at a cost of $100/person/month, because prices were negotiated through the UN-AIDS/WHO Initiative in 2001. In the richer countries, ART is available to citizens for free. The Saudi Arabian health department recently announced plans to build three AIDS-specific research and treatment facilities (United Press International 2004).

Yet, despite the investment in ART by some countries, prevention among high-risk groups lags far behind. Stigma and a social environment that marginalizes many of those at greatest risk continue to retard adequate responses and also have a negative influence on the development of adequate surveillance. To quote a recent publication by an expert group,

> *Even with recent declines in the price of antiretroviral therapy, lifetime costs for treating a case of HIV infection in a developing country will nevertheless be substantial. Unless the anticipated growth in new infections is prevented, the burden on treatment and care systems in low- and middle-income countries will be unsustainable over the long run, even with dramatically greater global assistance for the purchase and delivery of drugs. To preserve the hope of effective long-term treatment for the 40 million people currently living with HIV/AIDS, prevention efforts must be redoubled (Global HIV Prevention Working Group 2003, p. 22).*

While the possibility now exists for ART in many MENA countries, failure to integrate treatment with focused efforts to reduce stigma and eliminate taboos, and implement targeted prevention activities for high-risk groups, will result in costly and unsustainable treatment programs in the future. In this regard, the importance of having efficient surveillance systems to ensure evidence-based interventions cannot be overemphasized.

Private Sector

The private sector has barely been tapped to further HIV/AIDS prevention in the region. One exception that is known is the Coca Cola Foundation intervention in Egypt. It has made condoms available in selected workplaces and has conducted a study to design promotional and awareness campaigns. It is working with the UN Theme Group in Egypt where it hopes to pilot this program with eventual scale-up throughout North Africa.

Donor and Thematic Responses

UN Agencies

Since the beginning of 2002, more UN agencies have become active in the HIV/AIDS field. Both EMRO and UNAIDS now have several persons working at the regional level and are trying to improve staffing at the country level too. The United Nations Children's Fund (UNICEF), United Nations Development Programme (UNDP), and the United Nations Population Fund (UNFPA) now have regional posts specifically dedicated to HIV/AIDS. The United Nations Educational, Scientific, and Cultural Organization (UNESCO), International Labour Organization (ILO), and UNODC have begun to focus on HIV/AIDS in the region, although without increased dedicated staffing.

EMRO has held a series of meetings primarily on STIs, National AIDS Program (NAP) management and evaluation, the GFATM, counseling, and access to care. More recently, EMRO has prioritized treatment in the region as part of the global "3 by 5 Initiative," which aims to provide treatment access to 3 million infected persons worldwide by the end of 2005. In addition to its role in coordinating the UN response to HIV/AIDS, UNAIDS receives Program Acceleration Funds (PAF) for small projects. Information on those funds and their use in the MENA region (including the Sudan and Somalia) can be found in Annex 5.

While the general domain of action is set to some degree by each UN agency's global mission, specific strategies and activity plans have been slow to develop and reach the implementation stage. Several meetings have been held to decide what could be done and by whom. Overall, these meetings reflect a positive change in the region with the growing interest of UN agencies, the mobilization of some financial resources, and the desire to involve new national partners in the HIV/AIDS response. A global HIV Prevention Working Group estimated in 2003 that $23 million was devoted to HIV/AIDS programs during 2002 in the MENA region (as defined by UNAIDS) but that, to respond to the growing epidemic in the region, annual expenditures of $192 million would be required for HIV prevention activities by 2005, based on prevalence rates estimates for 2002 (Global HIV Prevention Working Group 2003). These figures indicate that mounting the kind of prevention response capable of preventing a significant outbreak of HIV/AIDS will require a tenfold increase in spending. It is important to note that those estimates were based on the insufficient data on the epidemic.

Vulnerable Populations—Prevention and Care

Despite continued indications of increasing risk factors, not much research has been conducted to investigate them and design appropriate interventions. The following summarizes the little research that has been conducted with regard to risk factors.

Injecting Drug Users

According to the Working Group mentioned above, less than 1 percent of IDUs in the region have access to harm reduction interventions that can substantially reduce the spread of HIV. Increasing numbers of HIV-positive cases have been detected in Libya and among Libyans visiting Tunisia since 2000, and UNODC is now sponsoring a rapid assessment on drug and HIV/AIDS in Libya. In Oman, the percentage of all HIV cases caused by IDU transmission has been rising. Although Oman has been quite open about its epidemic, no specific interventions for IDUs have been developed as yet. The Theme Group on HIV/AIDS in Algeria is conducting a rapid assessment response for IDU. Also in Egypt, UNODC has undertaken some preliminary outreach to IDUs in Cairo and Alexandria, identifying about 400 IDUs during the first attempt.

Prisons are frequently high-risk areas for the transmission of HIV, especially if IDUs are continuing to gain access to injectable drugs while in prison. The Islamic Republic of Iran has developed a model intervention that UNODC would like to extend to other countries. Both Algeria and Lebanon are also developing HIV/AIDS interventions in the prison setting.

Sex Workers and Their Clients

The Working Group indicates that, in MENA, only about 5 percent of CSWs and their clients have access to behavioral interventions that can prevent the spread of HIV. Very little work has been done with sex workers and almost none with their client groups. There was an outreach program for sex workers in Djibouti, and testing of sex workers has taken place in Algeria, Egypt, the Islamic Republic of Iran, Lebanon, Jordan, Morocco (including male sex workers), and Syria. However, there have been no attempts to develop sex worker programs using the known best practice approaches that include social development and empowerment. This is largely due to the official denial of their existence and legal persecution. The Islamic Republic of Iran has been taking the first tentative steps to develop an outreach program with street sex workers in Teheran. Registered sex workers in Tunisia (numbering about 300) are regularly tested and treated for STIs and provided with condoms. Of considerable concern is the growing level of commercial sex work in Iraq, with no efforts yet made to diminish the inevitable spread of HIV or STIs in such a conflict situation.

Men Who Have Sex with Men

The only countries in the region so far known to have been relatively open about MSM are Lebanon and Morocco, where both surveys and outreach have taken place. Through a local NGO, Lebanon has been developing an outreach intervention for MSM in some "cruising" areas of Beirut. Egypt has conducted research on MSM but has not organized an intervention directed to their needs. Special efforts may be needed to ensure equity in access to ART, care, and support for these marginalized groups. Regionwide, only a minority of MSM have access to behavioral interventions to curb the spread of HIV (Global HIV Prevention Working Group 2003).

Migrants/Mobile Populations/IDPs/Refugees

Discussions have taken place with the Organization of the Petroleum Exporting Countries (OPEC) regarding the possibility of funding two initiatives that would address the issues of HIV among people who move around in the region. One is the Horn of Africa Initiative, which includes Djibouti, Ethiopia, Eritrea, Somalia, Sudan, and the Republic of Yemen. The second is the Sahara Initiative, including Algeria, Libya, Mali, Mauritania, Morocco, Niger, and Tunisia. The International Organization for Migration is involved, and these efforts will deal with numerous issues, including legal and illegal migration through Tamanrasset, Algeria. Multiple issues exist regarding refugees with HIV, including their rights to medical care, their potential deportation, family support, and so on. Regular migrants, such as men leaving Egypt for work in the Gulf States, are mandatorily tested for HIV before they leave. This testing has been noted as an opportunity for HIV education, including the teaching of condom use skills.

Truck drivers, especially on the heavily trafficked transport corridor between Djibouti and Ethiopia, have high susceptibility to HIV/AIDS infection. Other mobile populations, such as fishermen, particularly in the Republic of Yemen, require attention too. Regional bodies, like the Gulf Cooperation Council, could be brought into discussions on these topics.

People Living with HIV/AIDS

Over the past few years, progress has been made in a few countries in bringing people living with HIV/AIDS (PLWHAs) into association with the NAPs, most markedly in Algeria, Djibouti, Egypt, the Islamic Republic of Iran, Lebanon, and Oman. In October 2003, at the 11th International Conference for People Living with HIV/AIDS in Kampala, Uganda, UNICEF sponsored the attendance of PLWHAs from Algeria, Egypt, the Islamic Republic of Iran, Lebanon, Oman, and Tunisia. The West Bank and Gaza is reported to have 22 PLWHAs for whom support is sought. To date, no PLWHA support mechanism has been developed in the Republic of Yemen or Libya and only a small program in Djibouti is in place. In Lebanon support groups are developed by doctors and social workers who are associated with NGOs.

Antidiscrimination laws for PLWHAs have not been developed in the region as yet and a considerable amount of work is required to develop enabling policies for migrants and refugees. One very encouraging recent exception is the permission granted by the MoH in Lebanon to provide ART to infected Palestinian refugees living within Lebanon's borders.

Children and Youth

Some formative research on youth and vulnerable populations has been conducted in Algeria, Djibouti, Jordan, Lebanon, Morocco, Syria, Tunisia, and the Republic of Yemen. Quality varies considerably, and it does not seem that these studies have identified the contexts and meanings of risk behaviors among youth in any country. UNFPA has funded an ongoing youth intervention in Tunisia. Collaborators include the Arab Boy Scouts, International Planned Parenthood Federation (IPPF), and other NGOs. The first interagency meeting on young people and children was held in December 2002 in Cairo. OPEC funded UNFPA for a literature review in Lebanon, Morocco, Syria, and the Republic of Yemen. UNICEF has begun to contribute to the effort.

UNICEF has been conducting policy reviews, covering conventions on reproductive and human rights that prioritize young people, communications, advocacy, and orphans. It is investing in a Web site with an information technology organization and has employed professional media staff with public health expertise. Another study has also been sponsored by UNICEF on policy and covenants regarding young people. With UNICEF's contribution, Jordan has embarked on a major education campaign among youth in and out of schools. UNICEF also sponsors KAP (knowledge, attitude, practice) studies on young people's issues.

UNESCO has been developing an HIV/AIDS curriculum for the education sector, which is very conservative. It has been trying to build relations between NAPs and the education departments of different countries. They are translating into Arabic materials on human rights and young people.

Further Challenges and Gaps

General Awareness

In the majority of countries, no ongoing national education efforts have taken place. The Islamic Republic of Iran is now developing such a campaign for the general public. When efforts have been made, the messages have been vague, as in Egypt, and are seldom repeated. While Tunisia has been able to promote the use of condoms using humor and cartoons, its efforts appear to have been primarily concentrated on youth. UNICEF is considering a communication strategy for the region.

In a few countries like Oman and Jordan, it is apparent from surveys among young adults that the majority of people have a minimal working knowledge about HIV/AIDS. However, that knowledge is typically lacking in specific information on how to prevent oneself from acquiring an infection (for example, abstinence until marriage, being faithful to a faithful uninfected partner, using condoms, and using clean new needles) and includes much misinformation as well, such as believing that HIV is transmittable through contact with objects. Most striking is the severe extent of stigma reflected in the findings of surveys wherever they are conducted in the region. The association of HIV with immoral behaviors has been promulgated so thoroughly that an enormous effort will be needed to counteract this. Unless stigma and discrimination are reduced, efforts to promote VCT, or offer ART, will be hampered, and few people will seek information from hotlines or other public sources.

It will not be possible to make progress in combating the epidemic unless AIDS becomes visible, stigma is challenged and people living with HIV are encouraged to play their part in a community-wide AIDS response. This requires resolve and courageous leadership at various levels, particularly by government and religious leaders (The Synergy Project/USAID 2003).

Advocacy

The interface between service providers, including NGOs, medical providers, and so on, and the actual affected community members (those already infected and those most likely to become infected, that is, CSWs, MSM, IDUs), is fraught with communication and rights and power-related problems. Advocacy to address the social and policy issues that provoke these problems has not yet been conceived. While most UN agencies are aware of the need to advocate for political leadership and commitment, efforts to confront what is considered to be politically too sensitive are still generally lacking. Giving voice to the most at-risk groups to solve their problems remains limited. One exception took place at a recent UNAIDS/UNODC meeting on IDUs, which several ex-IDUs attended.

In addition to these issues, advocacy will be needed to extend the overall response beyond the confines of health and will require multisectoral approaches. Ministries of education, transport, military, shipping, and ports—as well as those dealing with women, youth, and social welfare—must all be mobilized to participate appropriately in HIV/AIDS prevention and support.

Capacity Building

Capacity building has been discussed many times in the region, and has included suggestions made by regional expert networks, but little has been accomplished. No serious attempts have been made to engage academic institutions or individuals in much-needed research. In Egypt and Jordan, Family Health International (FHI) with USAID are providing technical assistance on VCT and other efforts. IPPF has some expertise, particularly with women and sex workers, but to date few existing NGOs or local community-based organizations (CBOs) have developed prevention programs aimed at the most at-risk groups in the community. Many consider such programs impossible, given the lack of legal support for IDUs, MSM, and CSWs. Technical work—such as conducting studies, training and supervising peer educators and outreach workers, and implementing a useful monitoring process—requires dedicated full-time staff with appropriate skills. These skills will have to be developed through capacity building activities in nearly all countries of the region.

Sexually Transmitted Infections and Reproductive Health

Millions of curable STIs occur in the region, with only a fraction actually recognized by the public health system and even fewer reported. In Morocco, for example, recent well-structured efforts to strengthen and decentralize STI surveillance and case management have resulted in estimates of 600,000 STIs per year. With support from FHI, the NAP in Egypt carried out an evaluation of selected reproductive infections in various Egyptian populations in Greater Cairo between 1999 and 2000. Findings reveal high prevalence of curable STDs, reaching 36.55 percent and 23.8 percent in a small group of CSWs and MSM, respectively. In addition, 8.3 percent of women attending family planning clinics, 5.35 percent of drug users, and 4 percent of women attending antenatal clinics had at least one STI (FHI, Ministry of Health and Population, US-AID 2002). The Egyptian study indicates the need for a strong national STI prevention and control strategy and for a doubling of efforts to address vulnerable and high-risk groups. Such efforts are needed in all countries.

Research, Monitoring, and Evaluation

Surveillance in the region is very weak and improving this situation requires a considerable investment over a long period of time, starting with an assessment of laboratory capacity. It may be possible to focus on the behavioral side of second-generation surveillance in that it is a less territorially defined area. Nonetheless, considerable investment in building capacity will be needed.

Systematic rapid assessment and response studies on drug use, focusing particularly on injectable drugs and those that can become injectable, are needed throughout the region. In 1999, UNODC (then known as the United Nations Office of Drug Control and Crime Prevention [UNOD-CCP]) sponsored a well-executed, thorough study with biomarkers in the Islamic Republic of Iran. Since then, others have been carried out in Egypt, Lebanon, and, more recently, Libya.

Few studies have been conducted that adequately explain the structure and functioning of the sex trade, the number of sex workers, the proportion of men in the population who access sex workers, their occupations, or other essential information for developing much-needed interventions.

Small studies have been carried out on MSM in a few countries, and even fewer have explored the contexts and meanings of risk behaviors and where they take place. Earlier anthropological literature documented a traditional form of transgender prostitution in Oman, but no follow up on this issue in any country has taken place. Given that the majority of MSM is composed of men for whom the male-to-male sexual act has no implication for identity, the numbers involved are far higher than those who openly espouse a gay or local transgendered identity label. These men nearly always also have sex with women and most are or will be married. Efforts to reach these men, albeit quietly and in a way not to threaten their safety, must be supported for the health of the general public.

M&E is an area in which, as yet, there is little capacity and the appropriate institutional framework has not yet been developed. The Bank has supported a national M&E officer in Djibouti and UNAIDS introduced such posts in Morocco and Sudan in 2004. There is renewed recognition of the need to move on this effort, as evidenced by GFATM grants that include strengthening M&E in selected countries. However, all countries should be encouraged to learn how to monitor and periodically evaluate their programs. M&E capacity building activities need to be planned in a coordinated manner by donor organizations and should not just be designed to meet individual reporting needs.

Summary and Key Messages

During the last few years, national responses have advanced to some extent in most countries. In several countries, a process has taken place through which plans have been made and resources acquired. But even where funds have been made available, capacity to use them remains underdeveloped. The major gaps in response that need support either at the national, donor, or area levels include the following:

- Increasing political will and commitment among leaders, raising awareness of the general populace to the dangers of HIV/AIDS, and targeting the high-risk groups that are the drivers of the transmission of the infections with specific interventions. Achieving this will entail creating an enabling policy environment, including reducing the stigma associated with the disease. In countries where NSPs are yet to be developed, this would be a critical first step.

- Strengthening country-level surveillance and information systems to better track the epidemic and target interventions to vulnerable groups in the region. Vulnerable groups that have been identified in the region are IDUs, CSWs and their clients, MSMs, prisoners, and the youth.

- Raising the priority given to HIV/AIDS research that should include analyzing the relevance of NSPs, readiness of countries to address the epidemic, cost of treatment, and care and prevention among other areas.

- Capacity building in all areas of HIV/AIDS programming including but not limited to the following areas: designing and implementing HIV/AIDS strategic plans, strengthening surveillance and research systems, encouraging multisectoral collaboration, working with NGOs, and designing and implementing quality interventions targeted at-risk groups and M&E.

Note

1. Algeria, Djibouti, the Arab Republic of Egypt, the Islamic Republic of Iran, Jordan, Lebanon, Libya, Morocco, Oman, Saudi Arabia, Syria, Tunisia, West Bank and Gaza, and the Republic of Yemen.

References

Family Health International (FHI), Ministry of Health and Population, USAID. 2002. Evaluation of Selected Reproductive Health Infections in Various Egyptian Population Groups in Greater Cairo. 1998–2000. Cairo: FHI.

Global HIV Prevention Working Group. May 2003. Access to HIV Prevention. Closing the Gap. Convened by Bill and Melinda Gates Foundation and the Henry J. Kaiser Family Foundation. The Synergy Project/USAID. January 2003. HIV/AIDS Country Profile. Jordan.

United Press International, Saudi Arabia. 2004. "Saudi Arabia Builds AIDS Facilities." January 26.

CHAPTER 3

Strategic Directions

For low HIV/AIDS prevalence settings such as the MENA region, countries must be prepared to intervene at three key levels to keep prevalence rates low: advocacy, information/knowledge base and prevention. These three interventions must be implemented concurrently to be effective in keeping prevalence rates low. An enabling environment within which these interventions can take place is essential. Advocacy to raise the awareness of leaders regarding the issues, and reduce the stigmas associated with the disease is key to achieving this. Within an enabling environment, people at risk can be empowered to take greater control of their own lives and safety as it concerns the infection. Empowering people will require governments to reduce barriers (such as policies, regulations, customs and attitudes) at all levels that the populace face, which prevent them from adequately protecting themselves. Combining knowledge with reduced barriers and services will facilitate empowerment of individuals and communities in a way that they can alter risky practices and access needed services, leading to a reduction in transmission of HIV. Implementing effective prevention programs that incorporate these elements will require knowledge about the major factors that influence risk taking among those people whose lifestyles will likely expose themselves and others to HIV. While the infection is still largely confined to vulnerable groups, countries with low prevalence epidemics need to be ready to take advantage of the opportunity to create an enabling environment and to improve their information/knowledge base to implement prevention efforts among these groups. This would be much more effective and less costly than having to deal with a full-blown epidemic. While the strategy advocates keeping HIV prevalence rates low, the Bank also acknowledges the need to provide care and treatment for those already infected and needing these services. The strategy proposes to support these services within national HIV/AIDS strategic plans.

Key Strategic Directions

These strategic directions are based on the Bank's comparative advantage, numerous consultations with regional partners, and the business case for the Bank's engagement in this area. Based on these, the following four strategic directions for HIV/AIDS programming investments have been identified as areas in which the Bank can be strategically involved:

- Engage political leaders, policy makers, and key stakeholders to raise awareness and increase the priority given to HIV/AIDS programs within national and regional development agendas.

- Support the upgrading of surveillance systems and strengthen research and evaluation of epidemiological, economic, and behavioral aspects of HIV/AIDS to enhance the effectiveness of HIV/AIDS policies and programs.

- Support the development of national HIV/AIDS strategies and programs, based on the specific epidemiological, social, and economic conditions and the context of each country.

- Support capacity building and knowledge sharing for comprehensive management of HIV/AIDS programs.

These strategic directions fit within the conceptual framework that integrates advocacy, information, and prevention interventions needed in low prevalence areas. Because no single institution has all the resources and specialized skills required to address these needs, meeting them will require active partnership and collaboration among various stakeholders to assist governments to work in a comprehensive and harmonized approach. Based on the Bank's comparative advantage of being a financial institution, skilled in economic and social analysis, and being a convener of stakeholders and resources, the Bank is in a distinct position to coordinate efforts. Table 3.1 provides a snapshot of the role of the Bank in the four areas of need that have been identified.

As indicated in the table, within each area of need, the Bank's role varies as does the skills it will provide. These roles and skills will be discussed further under each specific strategic direction.

Strategic Direction 1

Engage political leaders, policy makers and key stakeholders to raise awareness and increase the priority given to HIV/AIDS programs within national and regional development agendas.

TABLE 3.1

World Bank's Role in Key Strategic Directions

Priority Areas/ Fit with Conceptual Framework	Roles		
	Leadership	Active Partnership	Participant
Engage political leaders and policy makers/ Advocacy	X (convener, economic analysis)		
Strengthen knowledge base/ Information and advocacy		X (economic and social analysis, financier[a])	
Support the development of national HIV/AIDS strategies/ Advocacy, information, and prevention			X (convener, financier)
Support capacity building/ Information and prevention		X (financier, economic and social analysis)	

a. Financing in terms of grants (for example, Institutional Development Fund, technical assistance grants, trust funds), credits (for International Development Association countries), or loans (for International Bank for Reconstruction and Development countries).

The major challenge to addressing HIV/AIDS in the region is to encourage political and social leadership to respond while the epidemic can still be contained and before the cost of care becomes very high. The Bank's role as a convener of key government stakeholders, coupled with the ability to implement economic analysis with which to guide governments' economic agendas, makes it feasible for the Bank to take a leadership role in this area. The objectives of the Bank's involvement are to:

- Raise awareness to the threat posed by the epidemic and support the creation of an enabling environment for HIV/AIDS programming, and

- Mobilize political/social commitment and action toward proactively responding to the epidemic while still at an early stage.

Approaches

- Support analytical work, as well as media and advocacy activities, to raise awareness among political leaders and other key stakeholders

- Undertake analytical work to evaluate the cost-effectiveness of different HIV/AIDS interventions and justify investments in HIV/AIDS programs

- Mobilize additional resources to support the design and implementation of priority HIV/AIDS programs

- Support policy dialogues with client counterparts during country assistance strategy (CAS), public expenditure review (PER), and poverty reduction strategy paper (PRSP) preparation; include HIV/AIDS in relevant national, subregional, and regional seminars and conferences

- Raise awareness among Bank staff about the importance of HIV/AIDS issues and communication options

By using various opportunities for policy and country dialogue available to management and staff of the region, the Bank can play a critical role in raising the importance of HIV/AIDS and placing it on the development agenda of client countries. Without political commitment at the highest levels from all concerned sectors, any HIV/AIDS program stands a good chance of failing. Bank regional management plays an important role and can use available communication tools and country dialogue opportunities to build the required commitment across all sectors of interaction.

Clearly, more analytical work will be required to support the effort to raise HIV/AIDS awareness, but the two activities must occur simultaneously. As the results of ongoing analysis become available, they can be integrated into policy dialogue tools and used to update messages to client countries.

Strategic Direction 2

Support the upgrading of surveillance systems and strengthen the research and evaluation of epidemiological, economic, and behavioral aspects of HIV/AIDS to enhance the effectiveness of HIV/AIDS policies and programs.

Working in active partnership with other partners with the required skills like UNAIDS and WHO, the Bank as a financier can provide the necessary resources to strengthen and scale up the second-generation surveillance systems needed to adequately track and monitor the epidemic. In the area of social and economic research, the Bank's skills can also contribute to supporting the knowledge base of the region about HIV/AIDS. The objectives of the Bank's involvement are as follows:

- Support institutional and local capacity development in the generation and use of essential data/information to plan and implement HIV/AIDS programs,

- Support the development of comprehensive M&E plans and the capacity to implement them, and

- Support and encourage collaboration and sharing of information.

Approaches

- Institute second-generation surveillance, including STD and behavioral surveys, especially among high-risk groups

- Conduct research on vulnerable groups, such as migrants, youth, IDUs, and CSWs, and identify constraints such as social stigma and behavioral factors that affect the mode of transmission

- Undertake the analysis of gender-specific vulnerabilities to HIV infection, and the impact of HIV/AIDS on women and their families, and identify appropriate policies and adjustments in existing laws and regulations to address these constraints

Surveillance methods currently in place can overlook outbreaks in marginalized social groups who tend to be the driving force of HIV epidemics when prevalence levels are low. Second-generation surveillance systems, which collect behavioral data that can reveal the epidemic as it emerges in the most at-risk groups and identify those who are potentially at risk in the immediate future, are largely absent in the region. Without this information, targeting effective interventions to the appropriate group is impossible and governments cannot understand their epidemic and monitor changes through time. Achieving the HIV/AIDS goal (as the other goals) of the MDGs requires evidenced-based and focused policies that can be put in place only when adequate data on the epidemic are available. Small investments could be made to improve current surveillance systems and build further knowledge about the current dynamics and epidemiological situation.

In second-generation surveillance, key vulnerable populations are sampled for HIV, in an unlinked anonymous manner, and for syphilis, in a linked though confidential manner, so that the person can be treated. Each key population should also be sampled in a statistically representative framework, with questionnaire surveys, to achieve the following:

- Provide timely information for advocacy and program planning

- Track changing risk behaviors (for example, condom use)

- Track the changing sociodemographic composition of these groups

- Reveal links among groups

- Inform future interventions and elaborate and improve on existing ones

- Explain any reductions (or rises) in STD or HIV prevalence

- Reveal multiple factors leading to vulnerability

- Suggest new groups for sero-surveillance

- Measure overall impact of existing interventions

National programs need in-depth information as well, gathered best by the inclusion of qualitative methods, both on the socioeconomic factors that contribute to HIV vulnerability and on the economic and societal impact of HIV/AIDS. This information feeds directly into the planning and design of multisectoral programs. Stigma, in particular, has been shown to be a major barrier to many of the actions needed to control the epidemic. When people fear the social and economic consequences of being exposed as HIV-positive, they avoid testing, support services, and treatment, and they are less easily persuaded to prevent further transmission. Diminishing stigma and discrimination in jobs, housing, and so on is an essential national function.

Understanding the gender dimensions of HIV/AIDS epidemics is key. With respect to CSWs, women are socially and biologically at greater risk of acquiring an HIV infection than men. Women suffer disproportionately as the caregivers and household managers after a spouse becomes infected. In the MENA region, family law systems should be reviewed to ensure that women are protected from loss of property and other disadvantages that increase poverty and destroy social safety mechanisms. With respect to MSM and IDUs, men are at greater risk. Sector work on the gender dimensions is needed and appropriate. The Gender and Development Unit of the Bank can support activities in this area.

Strategic Direction 3

Support the development of national HIV/AIDS strategies and programs, based on the specific epidemiological, social, and economic conditions and context of each country.

As one of the largest investors in the prevention and mitigation of HIV/AIDS in developing countries, an institution that works across sectors, levels, and regions and a convener of key stakeholders, the Bank can participate by promoting relevant multisectoral policies and approaches to develop national HIV/AIDS strategies and programs. The objectives of the Bank's involvement are as follows:

- Raise awareness to the multisectoral nature of the epidemic and strengthen intersectoral actions required to address the epidemic, and

- Ensure that all relevant Bank projects in the region are HIV/AIDS responsive.

Approaches

- Integrate the national HIV/AIDS strategy within national development plans and budget frameworks, including intersectoral programs and activities

- Support the NAP to mainstream HIV/AID activities in relevant key sectors

- Undertake systematic M&E of national HIV/AIDS programs to measure impact and improve effectiveness

- Within the Bank, include HIV/AIDS activities in the project preparation process for new projects and retrofit relevant ongoing projects with HIV/AIDS activities

As an issue of development, HIV/AIDS requires a more comprehensive response and approach than the usual health sector response that currently prevails in the region. The multisectoral nature of the Bank's responses (for example, economic, social, legal, transport, governance, infrastructure, rural development, and so on) is extremely relevant for successful HIV/AIDS programming. This comparative advantage of the Bank provides an opportunity to further promote multisectoral planning and partnerships within the Bank, in client countries and with other development partners. To promote greater harmonization of support to national HIV/AIDS strategies by various donors, this strategy proposes that the Bank adhere to the principles of the "three ones" in each country it intervenes. This principle advocates that for each country there should be—

- One agreed HIV/AIDS action framework that provides the basis for coordinating the work of all partners,

- One national AIDS coordinating authority, with a broad-based multisectoral mandate, and

- One agreed country level M&E system.

When these principles are not in place, the Bank and other partners can assist governments to implement them. It is important that Bank staff in the various sectors fully comprehend and appreciate the role of their various sectors in HIV/AIDS programming to be able to promote the same multi-sectoral approach in each client country. In this regard, country NSPs could be reviewed for their relevance to the epidemiological context and dynamics of each country. This would also promote relevant multisectoral policy and planning. Collaboration between the region and the World Bank Institute (WBI), other Bank regions, and the Bank's Global HIV/AIDS Unit will be necessary in raising awareness of sectoral staff on HIV/AIDS issues. In the Sub-Saharan region, for example, a number of HIV/AIDS projects are managed by non-health sectors. Their experiences could be tapped for similar approaches in the MENA region, where this is found to be appropriate.

Equally essential is the need to monitor and periodically evaluate the effectiveness of national programs. Investment without M&E is ineffective and inefficient, yet many national programs still have no adequate M&E systems. Commonly, there is little capacity to design or implement these systems. The local capacity to conduct all of these research functions must be supported with funding and technical assistance to build sustainability, a role that the Bank can play effectively.

A review of the region's project portfolio for inclusion of relevant HIV/AIDS activities will be a critical first step in a retrofitting exercise. Sharing the results of the review with various sectors will be a practical step for sectoral staff to appreciate the avenues to incorporate HIV/AIDS activities in ongoing projects. For new projects, incorporating HIV/AIDS activities can be mandated at the preparation phase, where appropriate, as has been institutionalized with environmental issues.

Strategic Direction 4

Support capacity building and knowledge sharing for the comprehensive management of HIV/AIDS programs.

Working in active partnership with other development agencies in the region, the Bank could provide the financial and technical resources required to support capacity building activities identified under the national and regional HIV/AIDS programs. The objective of the Bank's involvement is as follows:

- Raise awareness and develop capacity of Bank staff and relevant client country staff for better management of HIV/AIDS programs.

Approaches
- Develop multisectoral planning capacity to identify and design appropriate, cost-effective interventions that will reduce vulnerability among high-risk groups

- Mobilize resources at different levels to support capacity building in the region in close cooperation with UN agencies, NGOs, and representatives of the civil society

- Support the development of centers of excellence among key research institutions in the region to sustain training and capacity building activities over a longer term

- Within the Bank, collaborate with WBI and the Bank's Global HIV/ AIDS Unit on capacity building efforts for staff and client countries

Among the Bank's staff, greater technical understanding of HIV should be fostered in order for the Bank to accomplish its aims with regard to HIV/AIDS. Beyond mere awareness, client country staff should be familiar with all potential funding mechanisms, the best strategies and opportunities for countries in different phases of the epidemic, the range of preparatory activities required to design a sound national program, the common problems encountered when implementing these projects, and effective solutions. As a disease that is transmitted mainly through sex and drug use, behavior is a paramount issue in controlling the epidemic, and these behaviors are often considered immoral, illegal, and taboo. Helping Bank staff learn more about how to deal with this in a socially and culturally appropriate manner will enable them, in turn, to discuss these issues with country-based leaders and decision makers, using the best of international experience.

In this regard, WBI could design appropriate learning programs not only for MENA staff but also for client countries on a demand basis. A greater familiarity with the issues associated with HIV/AIDS, will enable the Bank staff in the MENA region to more effectively promote the interests of decision makers in seeking support for improved HIV/AIDS prevention and control.

Building sustainable capacity in the region will require collaboration with local and international institutions, foundations, and bilateral and multilateral donors to create mechanisms that will enable MENA actors to carry out the needed tasks of research, surveillance, implementation, and M&E. Capacity building will foster the development of centers of excellence, the growth of civil society, and the establishment of sound CBO and program management. The Bank can also organize and facilitate south-to-south technical exchanges and study tours between priority MENA NAPs and those from countries with similar HIV/AIDS epidemiological profiles that have sustained experience in addressing HIV/AIDS programmatically. Technical exchanges can support HIV/AIDS capacity building activities and can be tailored to meet the needs of the recipients of the exchanges. The exchanges would consist of sharing knowledge, lessons learned, experiences, successes, and failures in implementing HIV/AIDS programs and agendas.

Since efforts on all of the above key strategic directions take considerable time and resources, action must start now. The virus waits for no one.

Timeline, Geographic, and Area Priorities

Resources are not limitless. Therefore, timing of the Bank's involvement in the four key directions will need to be planned around resource constraints. However, some activities like engaging political leaders and strengthening the knowledge base, which can be easily integrated into ongoing Bank business, can take place in the short to medium term without much of an incremental budget. But others, such as supporting national HIV/AIDS strategies and programs and capacity building, will require additional resources and will have to be planned in the medium to long term. Another consideration for the timing of the Bank's involvement will be the availability in countries of other funding sources like grants from the GFATM. In such cases, the Bank can provide the needed technical assistance to implement programs in the short to medium term.

Because it will not be feasible for the Bank to support HIV/AIDS programming in all countries of the region at once, eligibility criteria have been developed to provide guidance on geographic priorities. Criteria and indicators for the Bank's involvement in HIV/AIDS programming in a country include the following:

- Ongoing dialogue between the Bank and the country and, as an extension, in cases in which CASs and PERs are being prepared

- Evidence of the government's commitment to address HIV/AIDS (such as the existence of a national HIV/AIDS strategic plan and dedicated resources) and the expressed interest of the country for the Bank to support its efforts

- Opportunity to work with other development partners (for example, UN Theme Group on HIV/AIDS) and to leverage technical and financial resources (for example, the existence of funds from GFATM)

- Ongoing World Bank projects/interventions in which HIV/AIDS activities can be retrofitted

- Presence of an enabling environment for the Bank to work in an intersectoral manner

Annex 6 provides a typology of potential MENA countries for the Bank's involvement. Based on the above criteria, this strategy has identified a number of countries where the available but limited resources can be put to specific use in the short to medium term. These countries are Djibouti,[1] the Islamic Republic of Iran, Jordan, Lebanon, Morocco, and the Republic of Yemen. Within these countries, the importance of each of the four strategic directions may vary depending on the country context. For example, in a country like Morocco where the government is already reasonably engaged in HIV/AIDS programming, the Bank's intervention should focus more on providing technical assistance to implement specific programs (that is, more focus on Strategic Directions 3 and 4 than on 1). Within the countries where the Bank intervenes, the priority groups that have been identified for focused interventions are IDUs, CSWs, prisoners, the youth, and MSM.

While other countries not included on this list can be added as more resources become available and request for the Bank's assistance increases, this strategy proposes that opportunities for advocating increased HIV/AIDS investments in these countries be fully utilized. Currently, there is insufficient information on the epidemic in the Gulf countries to make a case for more immediate interventions than continuing advocacy for action. When the Bank's support is requested in these countries, requests can be met through the World Bank Reimbursable Technical Assistance program.

Table 3.2 at the end of this chapter provides a synopsis of the MENA HIV/AIDS strategy.

Risks and Challenges Associated with Implementation of the Strategy

Successfully implementing this strategy comes with associated risks and challenges that need to be kept in mind and appropriately addressed. Below is a brief review of some of these challenges and suggestions about how they can be addressed.

- **Lack of Political Engagement:** Political will and commitment are essential for effective HIV/AIDS programming, without which it will be nearly impossible to achieve the political engagement required to involve all of the stakeholders in the task at hand. To address this challenge and to build the understanding necessary to convince political leaders of the need to engage in HIV/AIDS prevention programs while the prevalence rates are low, the right types of data on the epidemic and its potential impact must be acquired.

- **Weak Surveillance System and Insufficient Data:** Without data with which to ascertain the actual HIV/AIDS prevalence levels in the general population and in high-risk groups (as well as their patterns of interaction), planning, implementing, and monitoring an effective HIV/AIDS program will be an exercise in futility. The Bank can strengthen surveillance systems as well as encourage local research to improve the regional knowledge base on the epidemic and on viable options to address this challenge.

- **Denial and Stigma:** Many countries in the region are still very much in denial of the presence and potential impact of HIV/AIDS on their country's economy and development. There is the general belief that low prevalence equates to low risk and the protective role of culture and religious beliefs in preventing the spread of the infection. The persistence of denial and stigma associated with the disease presents a challenge to developing the enabling environment necessary to keep HIV/AIDS prevalence levels low. While it is acknowledged that addressing stigma is a difficult and long-term process, a critical first step to address this challenge will be to invest in improved surveillance and research to provide the evidence needed to convince policy makers and civil society stakeholders of the need for action.

- **Resource Limitations:** These limitations include the financial and human resources needed to mount effective HIV/AIDS programs. Although some countries have already embarked on mobilizing the needed financial resources (for example, through the GFATM), most countries still face the added problem of a severe lack of experienced human resources to plan and implement their HIV/AIDS programs. Investment in capacity building by the Bank and other development partners is very much needed by all countries of the region. In situations in which financial resources are also lacking, the Bank can play a role through lending and grant mechanisms.

- **Innovation and Flexibility:** The level of denial and stigma associated with HIV/AIDS in the region indicates that some level of creative innovativeness will be required to cultivate the essential enabling environment for effective programs to address the epidemic. The need for greater flexibility of the Bank's instruments of assistance will be a challenge to operationalize these innovations. Addressing this challenge will likely require a case-by-case review as has been done in other regions.

Conclusion and Key Message

Although available evidence indicates that the HIV/AIDS prevalence levels in the region are low, actual levels in the general population and in high-risk groups are not known with any degree of certainty. Ascertaining these facts is a critical first step in designing evidence-based interventions that can prevent the further spread of HIV/AIDS in the region. Persuading client country governments and other stakeholders will require better data on the HIV/AIDS situation in each country. These interventions can be implemented effectively only within the context of an overarching enabling environment for which greater political commitment is critical. The MENA Region of the Bank has a unique opportunity and an important role to play to ensure that these interventions are implemented by mobilizing multiple sectors and adapting various Bank instruments already in use in other regions.

Key Message: low prevalence does not mean low risk and action now can prevent a probable epidemic. The region is lagging in its defense against this devastating epidemic, but it may also have the advantage of time. Timing is crucial and the opportunity that exists now must not be wasted if the mistakes made in other regions with more advanced stages of the epidemic are to be avoided in the MENA region.

TABLE 3.2

Synopsis of MENA Regional HIV/AIDS Strategy

Strategic Direction	Objective	Approach	Key Expected Benefits
1: Engage political leaders, policy makers, and key stakeholders to raise awareness and increase the priority given to HIV/AIDS programs within national and regional development agendas.	• To raise awareness to the threat posed by the epidemic and support the creation of an enabling environment for HIV/AIDS programming. • To mobilize political and social commitment and action toward proactively responding to the epidemic while still at an early stage.	• Support analytical work, media, and advocacy activities to raise awareness among political leaders and other key stakeholders. • Undertake analytical work to evaluate the cost-effectiveness of different HIV/AIDS interventions and justify investments in HIV/AIDS programs. • Mobilize additional resources to support the design and implementation of priority HIV/AIDS programs. • Support policy dialogue with client counterparts during CAS, PER, and PRSP preparation and inclusion of HIV/AIDS in relevant seminars and conferences. • Raise awareness among Bank staff on the importance of HIV/AIDS issues	• Increased commitment of governments to HIV/AIDS programming. • Inclusion of HIV/AIDS in policy dialogue tools (CAS, PER, PRSP, and so on). • Enabling environment and government policies that support the scaling up of HIV/AIDS activities.
2: Support the upgrading of surveillance systems and strengthen the research and evaluation of epidemiological, economic, and behavioral aspects of HIV/AIDS to enhance the effectiveness of HIV/AIDS policies and programs.	• To support institutional and local capacity development in the generation and use of essential data/information for planning and implementing HIV/AIDS programs. • To support the development of comprehensive M&E plans and the capacity to implement them. • To support and encourage collaboration and sharing of information.	• Institute second-generation surveillance, including STD and behavioral surveys. • Conduct research on vulnerable groups, and identify constraints such as social stigma and behavioral factors that affect the mode of transmission. • Undertake analysis of gender-specific vulnerabilities to HIV infection, and the impact of HIV/AIDS on women and their families, and identify appropriate policies and adjustments in existing laws and regulations to address these constraints.	• Improved quality of HIV/AIDS surveillance systems and data leading to informed policy decisions. • HIV/AIDS programs incorporating key gender concerns. • Vulnerability, risky behaviors, and at-risk groups identified for targeted outreach HIV/AIDS programs.

continued

TABLE 3.2

Synopsis of MENA Regional HIV/AIDS Strategy—*continued*

Strategic Direction	Objective	Approach	Key Expected Benefits
3: Support the development of national HIV/AIDS strategies and programs, based on the specific epidemiological, social, and economic conditions and context of each country.	• To raise awareness on the multisectoral nature of the epidemic and strengthen intersectoral actions required to address the epidemic. • To ensure that all relevant Bank projects in the region are HIV/AIDS responsive.	• Integrate the national HIV/AIDS strategy within national development plans and budget frameworks, including intersectoral programs and activities. • Support the National AIDS Programs to mainstream HIV/AIDS activities in relevant key sectors. • Undertake systematic M&E of national HIV/AIDS programs to measure impact and improve effectiveness. • Within the Bank, include HIV/AIDS activities in the project preparation process for new projects and retrofit relevant ongoing projects with HIV/AIDS activities.	• National and regional HIV/AIDS plans and actions involving all key development sectors. • M&E systems for HIV/AIDS developed in countries. • HIV/AIDS mainstreamed in relevant projects and tasks.
4: Support capacity building and knowledge sharing for comprehensive management of HIV/AIDS programs.	• To raise awareness and develop the capacity of Bank staff and relevant client country staff for better management of HIV/AIDS programs.	• Develop multisectoral planning capacity to identify and design appropriate, cost-effective interventions that will reduce vulnerability among high-risk groups. • Mobilize resources at different levels to support capacity building in the region in close cooperation with UN partners. • Support the development of centers of excellence among key research institutions in the region to sustain training and capacity building activities over a longer term. • Within the Bank, collaborate with WBI and the Bank's Global HIV/AIDS Unit on capacity building efforts for staff and client countries.	• Bank and key government staff enabled to plan and implement HIV/AIDS programs. • Local NGOs enabled to implement relevant and effective HIV/AIDS programs. • Capacity of regional research institutions strengthened in the area of HIV/AIDS research and training.

Note: CAS, Country Assistance Strategy; M&E, monitoring and evaluation; NGO, nongovernmental organization; PER, Public Expenditure Review; PRSP, Poverty Reduction Strategy Paper; STD, sexually transmitted disease; WBI, World Bank Institute.

Note

1. Assistance to Djibouti will likely vary from other countries, because it is already well funded with a stand-alone HIV/AIDS project. Therefore, Bank assistance will be more likely to focus on synergizing the experience of Djibouti with other countries of the region.

Economic Analysis of HIV/AIDS in MENA

Introduction

HIV/AIDS has now emerged as one of the world's worst infectious diseases. Virtually unknown 20 years ago, the epidemic has spread with ferocious speed to become the leading cause of death in Africa. Other regions and countries, which once were thought to be immune to the spread of HIV/AIDS, such as Russia, India, and China, now stand on the brink of widespread epidemics.

Countries in the Middle East and North Africa (MENA) region are at an early stage of the HIV/AIDS epidemic with an average rate of prevalence of about 0.3 percent among the adult population. While these numbers are relatively low compared with Africa and Asia, low prevalence rate does not mean low risk. Recent evidence suggests that the number of adults and children living with HIV/AIDS is rising rapidly (see figure 1.1 in Chapter 1).

Based on the available information, HIV transmission is taking place mainly among high-risk groups such as injecting drug users (IDUs) and commercial sex workers (CSWs). But because of the lack of adequate surveillance data, outbreaks in such groups can easily be overlooked and spread to the general population as has happened elsewhere. Despite specific social and cultural values that have helped prevent the rapid spread of HIV/AIDS in MENA, the region exhibits high risks of vulnerability. The option of waiting to act until the HIV prevalence rate rises further in the general population would be a costly option. By that time, a general epidemic could be on its way and, as shown by the international evidence, it could then be too late to prevent the inevitable increase in human sufferings as well as associated losses in economic growth.

An Invisible but Lethal Disease

Most MENA countries are at an early stage of the HIV infection stage. However, the situation varies considerably across countries (box A1.1). Until recently, most cases of infection in MENA countries were found among IDUs, men who have sex with men (MSM), CSWs and their clients, prisoners (who are frequently drug users), and patients with sexually transmitted diseases (STDs).

As has happened in other countries, MENA countries face a risk that the HIV infection could spread to the general population. In Sub-Saharan Africa, the region hit hardest by HIV/AIDS, the epidemic spread mainly through heterosexual contacts and it has now reached an advanced AIDS stage. In Asia and the Pacific, injecting drug use combined with unprotected sex, rising rates of STDs, and other factors have led to an acceleration of the spread of HIV. While sociocultural factors have helped slow down the initial spread of HIV/AIDS in Asia, they have not prevented its increase. At one point in time, it was thought that an HIV/AIDS epidemic could not occur in India because its conservative values would prevent the spread of HIV. Yet, India now probably has the largest HIV positive population in the world.[1] In Eastern Europe and

---

BOX A1.1

Epidemiological Profiles in the MENA Region

Type 1: Repeated testing, consistently low rates, but no consistent testing or reporting of high-risk groups:

* Egypt, Jordan, Syria, and possibly Saudi Arabia and Iraq.

Type 2: Gradually growing accumulation of levels of infection and at least some rapid increases in identified high-risk groups:

* Algeria, Bahrain, the Islamic Republic of Iran, Kuwait, Lebanon, Libya, Morocco, Oman, the Republic of Yemen, Tunisia, and possibly Qatar and the United Arab Emirates.

Type 3: Generalized epidemic levels of HIV:

* Djibouti.

Source: Jenkins, C., and David A. Robalino. 2003. HIV/AIDS in the Middle East and North Africa: The Costs of Inaction. World Bank.

Central Asia, the rapidly growing epidemic is fueled by injecting drug use and secondarily by sexual transmission.

What makes the HIV/AIDS epidemic particularly lethal is that it remains invisible for a long period of time. In contrast to most other epidemics, which are of relatively short duration,[2] a long incubation period of five to eight years separates HIV infection from the AIDS stage. In the absence of adequate surveillance systems as is the case in most MENA countries, there are no early warning systems that would alert public health officials to detect outbreaks among high-risk populations.[3] Such a situation allows the HIV infection to spread from high-risk groups to the general population, at which point it is too late to prevent a generalized HIV/AIDS epidemic. The result is to transform a public health issue into a disease that affects the economic and social course of countries for many decades to come.

Long-Term Erosion of the Process of Economic Growth

The relationship between HIV/AIDS and economic development is complex. Long-wave events such as HIV/AIDS typically unfold over several decades rather than just a few years. This means that there is a long and uneven lag between the onset of the infection and the moment when the economic and social impacts become visible. At the macro level, the impact of the HIV/AIDS epidemic is felt through three main channels. The first one concerns the labor force. As people fall ill, they are less likely to be able to work and be productive. Because AIDS kills people in the prime of their working lives, the epidemic has a direct impact on output. But this impact depends on the structure of the labor market. In countries where there is a large pool of unemployed labor, the reduction in output would be small as firms could replace lost labor quickly. Over time, however, unemployment would fall and the economic impact of HIV/AIDS would be felt over the medium to long term.

The second economic impact affects human capital. Increased mortality affects not only unskilled labor but also skilled labor, which depletes the stock of human capital. In addition, it reduces the accumulation of human capital. As people live shorter lives, they have fewer incentives to invest in human capital and training. In particular, orphans are found to be less likely to be kept in school.

HIV/AIDS also affects the transmission of knowledge from adults to the younger generation. As the HIV epidemic creates an unprecedented number of orphans, it affects the process whereby the young generation learns its skills from the older generation. These effects were recently analyzed by constructing an overlapping generation model with two family structures, nuclear and pooled in the case of South Africa[4] and Kenya.[5] In a pooled family structure, children are raised by the extended family. Where this collective responsibility can no longer be assured because of the loss of parents because of HIV/AIDS, the transmission of knowledge from one generation to the next is weakened. When these orphans become adults, their capacity to transmit knowledge are also reduced, which erodes economic and social development.

The third impact of HIV/AIDS is to reduce savings and the accumulation of physical capital. Faced with increased AIDS-related expenditures and lower income caused by the illness of adult family members, households cut down on consumption and savings, which results in less investment and slower economic growth. Until recently, the reduction of savings because of AIDS was probably negligible. But this could be changing with the introduction of antiretroviral therapy (ART), which, even at the current lower prices, results in a large increase in per capita expenditures.

Overall, the economic impact of HIV/AIDS is felt by firms, households, and governments in the form of an "AIDS" tax. The tax is incurred by firms in the form of additional hiring and training cost (to replace lost labor), increased absenteeism, and higher medical claims and pensions. The resulting costs can be substantial as shown by the example of South Africa.[6] Given the high level of the tax, firms have an incentive to shift the burden of the tax either to households or to governments. This is accomplished by pre-employment screening, reducing the medical benefits and pensions paid by firms, outsourcing activities, and increasing the proportion of temporary workers. In the end, however, the AIDS tax still has to be paid by households and it reduces economic growth.

The AIDS tax is also borne by governments. Government revenues tend to decline as the size of the active labor force is reduced and individual productivity falls. In particular, HIV/AIDS reduces the productivity of the civil service, which weakens the capacity of governments to deliver essential services such as education and health. At the same time, AIDS-related expenditures increase. For MENA countries, the financial cost of HIV/AIDS can be substantial, especially when the AIDS stage is reached. As shown by Figure A1.1, the cost of HIV/AIDS prevention, treatment, and care could reach 1.5 percent of GDP on average by 2015.[7] As a result of lower revenues and increased AIDS-related expenditures, fewer resources are available for financing non-health expenditures, particularly investments, which reduces long-term economic growth.

What confers to HIV/AIDS such a devastating impact on countries is not only the direct effect of HIV/AIDS on economic growth, but also the reverse causality that can arise from development to HIV/AIDS in the absence of HIV prevention programs. Such causality is particularly strong when growth is accompanied by an increased number of migrant

FIGURE A1.1

HIV/AIDS-Related Health Expenditures in 2015

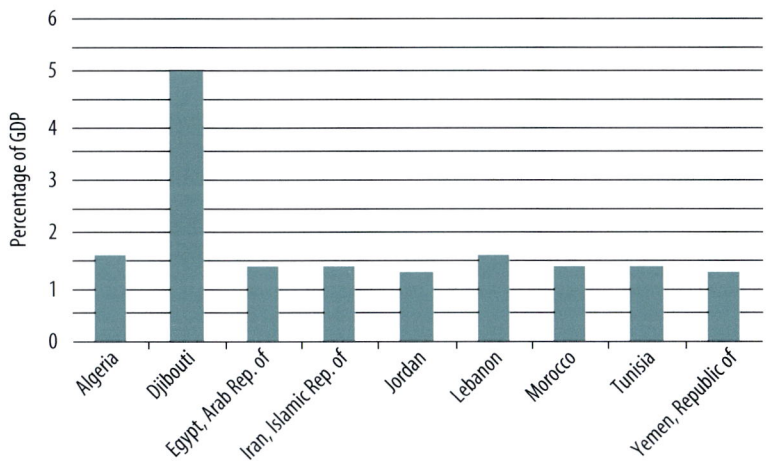

Source: Jenkins, C., and David A. Robalino. 2003. *HIV/AIDS in the Middle East and North Africa: The Costs of Inaction.* World Bank.

Note: GDP, gross domestic product.

labor, investments in large projects that depend on migrant labor, substantial political and social changes (as occurs in countries in transition from civil unrest), and an unequal process of economic development within a country. As shown by recent economic research at the household and community levels, such factors of vulnerability play a key role in accounting for the strength of the spread of HIV among countries.

Factors of Vulnerability

Level of income

Vulnerability to HIV/AIDS is likely to be much worse for low-income than high-income countries. High-income countries are in a better position to replace lost skills quickly and to avoid premature AIDS-related death. They can take advantage of a widespread medical infrastructure to dispense the medication that can allow HIV-infected individuals to remain engaged in economic activities. Because of their well-developed education system, high-income countries are also in a better position to replace lost skills than low-income countries. Alternatively, they can import skilled labor. On balance, MENA countries are medium to high income, and because of that they face lower vulnerability than low-income countries. For these countries the loss of human capital entails a high cost because of the scarcity of skills and the time involved in replacing them. However, medical costs may have a medium to low impact on the domestic savings of low-income countries, especially if they have access to grants to finance them.

Openness of countries

For both low- and high-income countries the economic impact of HIV/AIDS is likely to be worse the more open these economies are. In open economies the domestic rate of return to capital is linked to the world interest rate with an adjustment for country risk. As a result, foreign investors will be less inclined to invest in firms whose costs of operation are increased because of the cost of the HIV/AIDS epidemic, and domestic residents will face stronger incentives to invest abroad. Both effects amplify the economic costs of HIV/AIDS compared with a closed economy (Table A1.1).[8] Given the openness of MENA countries and the role of migration and tourism, MENA countries face high vulnerability risks.

Labor migration

While migration per se is not a risk factor, it is an important factor of vulnerability for MENA countries. The conditions under which migrants live often increase vulnerability and can trigger an increase in high-risk behavior. Preventing infection in this group is a long-term investment that has substantial benefits given the importance of migration for the region. For example, the Arab Republic of Egypt records some 3 million of migrant workers, most of them working in the Gulf countries. Algeria, the Islamic Republic of Iran, Jordan, Lebanon, Libya, Morocco, Syrian Arab Republic, and Tunisia also report high levels of migration. From the

TABLE A1.1

Economic Impact of HIV/AIDS in Rich and Poor Countries

Economic Impact through the following:	Low-Income Countries	High-Income Countries
Labor effects (loss of labor, reduction in productivity)	High	Low
Loss of acquisition and transmission of knowledge	High	Low
Impact on domestic savings and physical capital because of AIDS-related expenditures	Medium	Low/negligible
Openness of economies	High	High

Source: M. Haacker, "Modeling the Macroeconomic Impact of HIV/AIDS." IMF Working Paper, WP/2/195. 2002.

point of view of the receiving countries, migrant workers also form a large population group such as in Oman (25 percent of the total population are foreigners) or Saudi Arabia (850,000 Filipinos).

Governance factors

A key factor explaining why some countries have been able to mount an effective response to the HIV/AIDS epidemic early on is whether governments are accountable to the broad majority of the population. From this perspective, both the limited role of nongovernmental organizations (NGOs) and the difficult interaction between governments and civil society are factors that are likely to reduce the effectiveness of HIV/AIDS prevention programs in most countries. Additional factors include political instability and civil conflict in some countries.

Income inequality

Overall, there is a strong relationship between income inequality and the spread of HIV/AIDS (figure A1.2). Compared with other developing

FIGURE A1.2

Income Inequality and HIV Prevalence Rate in Developing Countries

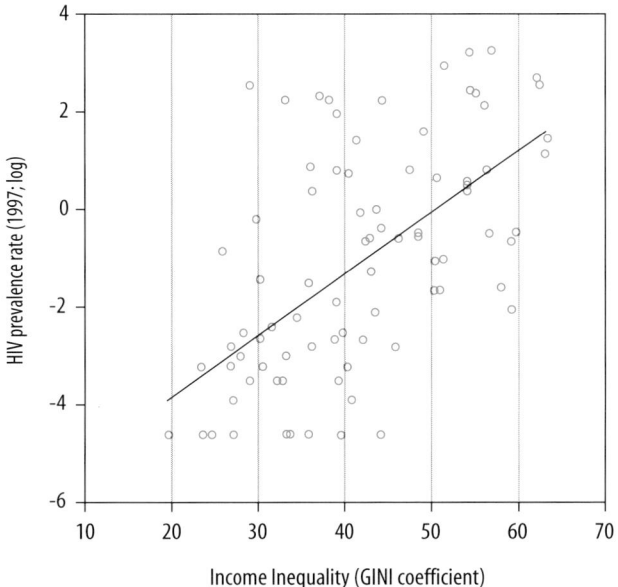

Source: Data from *World Development Indicators* (World Bank, 2001).

countries, North African countries would seem to have lower vulnerability because of their lower rates of inequality. Among other MENA countries, the Islamic Republic of Iran would seem to have a relatively high vulnerability risk. However, these indicators hide wide variations among countries. For example, although the total proportion of Moroccans living in poverty is estimated at between 13 percent and 16 percent, some 60 percent of rural Moroccans are estimated to be poor. This disparity fuels high levels of internal migration, which increases the vulnerability of migrant workers to HIV/AIDS. A similar result also characterizes other MENA countries such as Algeria.

Gender issues

Economic and social inequalities between men and women are perhaps one of the major factors of vulnerability to HIV/AIDS. As shown by figures A1.3 and A1.4, HIV prevalence rates are lower when women have access to education and significant economic opportunities to remain financially independent, respectively. These are areas that create significant risks of vulnerability for MENA countries. Countries in the region with high gender-related vulnerability risks include Djibouti, Iraq, Morocco, Saudi Arabia, Syria, and the Republic of Yemen.[9]

FIGURE A1.3

HIV/AIDS and Female Education in Developing Countries

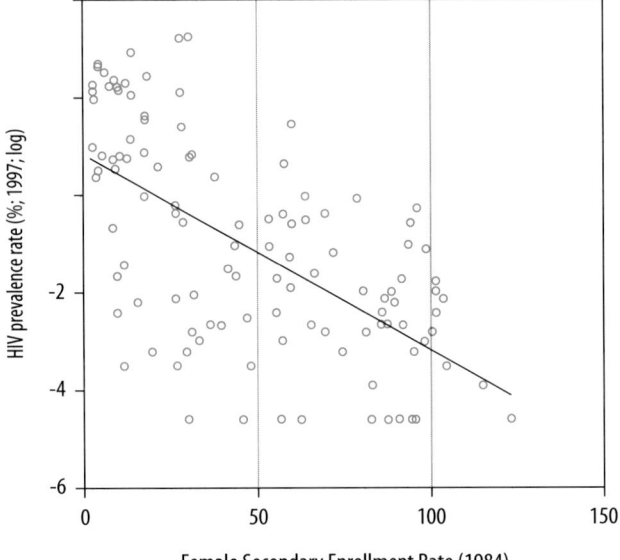

Female Secondary Enrollment Rate (1984)

Source: Data from *World Development Indicators* (World Bank, 2001).

Access to information

While education increases the incentive to invest in protective measures, their effects are unlikely to materialize unless adequate information on HIV/AIDS is provided. This is an area of substantial shortcoming in MENA countries. Few of the messages and materials provided by AIDS programs are clear, give explicit information about risk, or even mention the use of condoms for prevention. Not surprisingly, the broad lack of understanding of HIV/AIDS reported by various surveys of knowledge about HIV/AIDS is translated into a lack of protective behavior.

Cultural and social values

Values set apart MENA countries. On the one hand, social values and a strong role of the extended family system are reducing the vulnerability of society to HIV/AIDS. Similarly, the wide spread practice of circumcision also acts to reduce the spread of HIV/AIDS. On the other hand, the silence surrounding sexual issues is creating a strong risk factor as it limits the possibility of introducing sexual education in schools and setting up prevention measures. It also tends to drive people living with HIV/AIDS and high-risk groups deeper underground, which further

FIGURE A1.4

Female Employment and HIV/AIDS Prevalence Rate

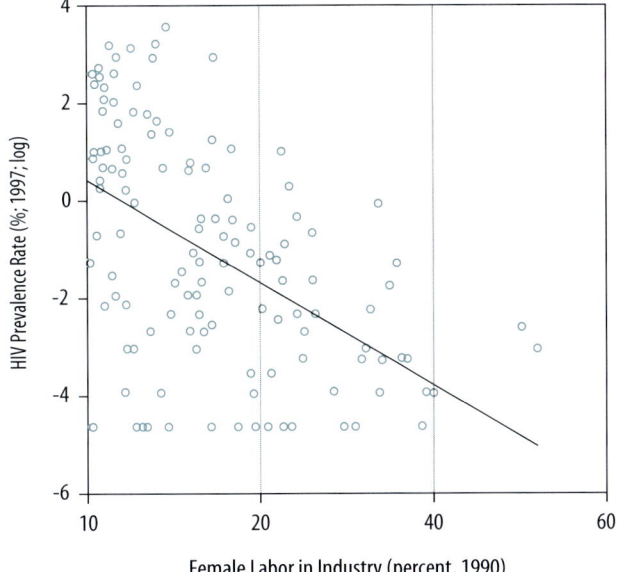

Source: Data from *World Development Indicators* (World Bank, 2001).

complicates the task of epidemiological surveillance. In addition, the rise of religious extremism may strengthen even more denial that there is an urgent need to implement prevention measures, particularly among high-risk groups. In such an environment, religion tends to be presented as a shield that is strong enough to prevent HIV/AIDS. Yet, as shown by the experience of Senegal in Western Africa, Muslim leaders can be enrolled to help halt the spread of HIV/AIDS.

Health and education infrastructure

This is one area where MENA countries are better placed, because most of their population have access to both education and health services. Such coverage makes it possible to reach the youth population—for example, through sexual education in schools—as well as to deliver effective prevention and treatment through the health system.

What is the net effect of these various risk factors?

Some evidence of the role of the various socioeconomic risk factors that affect the spread of the epidemic is provided by the analysis of Jenkins and Robalino.[10] Not surprisingly, these macrolevel indicators explain only part of the cross-country variation in the HIV prevalence rate given the poor quality of the available data. Nonetheless, the results provide some useful information on the factors that are likely to influence the diffusion of the epidemic in MENA countries.

When the model[11] developed for this analysis is applied to MENA countries, it predicts higher prevalence rates than the official estimates indicate. Based on current levels of output per capita, participation of women in the labor force, the levels of income inequality and rates of female illiteracy, HIV prevalence rates are found to be between 0.2 and 1 percentage point higher than current official estimates. For most countries this implies a near doubling of current HIV prevalence rates. The difference between the predicted rates and the official estimates could be a result of measurement issues (weak surveillance systems) or other sociocultural factors not considered and controlled for by the model. In any case the important conclusion is that prevalence rates are not likely to be lower than the current ones.

Economic Costs and Benefits of the HIV/AIDS Program

To evaluate the economic cost of HIV/AIDS in MENA, we use the results generated by combining a model of economic growth and an

FIGURE A1.5

Potential Underestimation of HIV/AIDS Prevalence Rates in MENA Countries

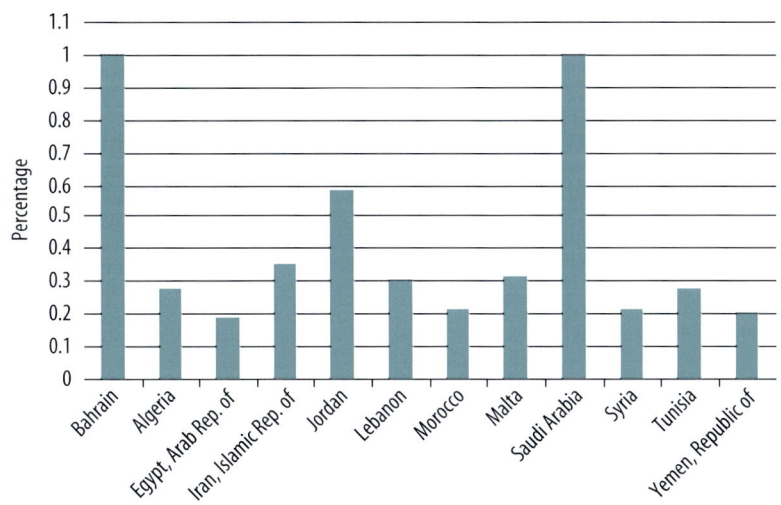

Source: Jenkins, C., and David A. Robalino. 2003. *HIV/AIDS in the Middle East and North Africa: The Costs of Inaction.* World Bank.

HIV/AIDS diffusion component.[12] The period of analysis is 2000–25. The impact of the epidemic on the economy is estimated by focusing on the following four channels: size and composition of labor force, productivity growth, health expenditures, and the savings rate of the economy. Three types of labor (skilled, unskilled, and unemployed) are considered. Other channels such as the reduction in human capital are ignored for methodological reasons. To that extent, the model underestimates the economic impact of HIV/AIDS.

The diffusion of HIV/AIDS is formalized by focusing on two channels of transmission: the sharing of infected needles among IDUs and through sexual intercourse. The population is divided into five groups: CSWs, female IDUs, male IDUs, low-risk females, and low-risk males. Given the high levels of uncertainty affecting the transmission parameters, a traditional simulation approach in which outcome variables are projected on the basis of explanatory variables would not be appropriate. Instead, the evolution of the HIV/AIDS epidemic and the economy is simulated by running 100 combinations of the various parameters that determine the course of the epidemic. These include the shares of high-risk population (IDUs and CSWs); the HIV/AIDS prevalence rates among these groups; the frequency and heterogeneity of sexual interactions; the prevalence of STDs; the prevalence of condom use and needle sharing; the distribution of AIDS-related deaths among the unemployed, skilled, and unskilled workers; and the reduction in total factor productivity growth resulting from HIV/AIDS.

The model is necessarily a simplification of the complex mechanisms through which the economy and the HIV/AIDS epidemic interact. Nonetheless, it captures the main effects of the epidemic on the labor force, productivity growth, health expenditures, and domestic savings rate.

What are the main results? First, the level of uncertainty surrounding the evolution of the HIV/AIDS epidemic is considerable. There are, however, quite a large number of scenarios clustered around an HIV/AIDS prevalence rate of around 4 percent by 2015. This result is important, because it is usually found that once the epidemic reaches such a level, its demographic and economic impacts become quite substantial. In the case of the MENA countries, the model generates a similar outcome. On average, the annual GDP growth rate for the 2000–25 would be reduced by 0.3 to 0.4 percentage points for all countries with the exception of Djibouti (-1.3 percentage points) (table A1.2)[13]. In total, the accumulated cost of the HIV epidemic for the period 2000–25 would amount to between 25 percent (the United Arab Emirates) and 54 percent (Tunisia) of current GDP and greater than 150 percent in the case of Djibouti. These are substantial costs that are incurred even though most of the economies currently have high unemployment rates. Costs would even be higher if the effect of HIV/AIDS on the accumulation of capital had been counted in the estimates.

TABLE A1.2

Economic Impact of the HIV/AIDS Epidemic

	Present Value Losses in 2000-25 (% of current GDP)	Average Reduction in GDP Growth Rate (%)	Average HIV Prevalence Rate in 2015[a]
Algeria	41.2	-0.40	4.5
Djibouti	150.8	-1.34	15.9
Egypt, Arab Rep. of	51.3	-0.42	4.2
Iran, Islamic Rep. of	38.7	-0.42	4.2
Jordan	33.6	-0.35	3.7
Lebanon	30.0	-0.45	4.6
Morocco	39.5	-0.42	4.3
Tunisia	54.0	-0.44	4.4
Bahrain	35.6	-0.38	4.2
Kuwait	35.7	-0.36	4.1
Oman	35.6	-0.35	4.0
Qatar	33.2	-0.38	4.3
Saudi Arabia	35.8	-0.31	3.7
United Arab Emirates	25.6	-0.32	3.9

Source: Jenkins, C., and David A. Robalino. 2003. *HIV/AIDS in the Middle East and North Africa: The Costs of Inaction.* World Bank.

a. The figures are calculated as averages across the scenarios that are generated.

Policy Implications

In principle, allocating public funds for an epidemic such as HIV involves a decision process quite similar to any other decisions about the use of public funds. It entails comparing the cost today of implementing a program of HIV/AIDS activities with the enhanced economic and social development that would be made possible by the subsequent reduction of the prevalence of HIV/AIDS. In the case of MENA countries, the choice they face is quite straightforward: either pay a small cost now to implement intervention measures or defer action and incur a much higher cost in the future. Because the epidemic is still at an early stage, the intervention measures would consist mainly of improved surveillance activities (to remedy the current shortcomings of the current system), prevention activities targeting specific groups, and information and education campaigns (IEC).

Key high-risk target groups

High-risk groups include the following:

- **IDUs and their sex partners.** Most IDUs in the region are males and nearly one-third are married. Condom use among IDUs is, however, rare, which creates strong risk of spread of HIV/AIDS.

- **Prison inmates.** In the Islamic Republic of Iran, for example, some 10 percent of inmates are reported to inject drugs (UNAIDS 2004) with 90 percent sharing needles with others. By 2001, 12.5 percent of prison inmates were estimated to be HIV positive (UNAIDS 2004, epidemic update; Global HIV Prevention Working Group, 2003).

- **Other social groups.** Although there is a general lack of information concerning the high-risk social groups, various surveys have detected infection rates among MSMs and CSWs and their clients (Jenkins and Robalino 2003; UNAIDS 2004, epidemic update).

For all these high-risk groups there is an urgent need to act now. This need is highlighted by the broad lack of preventive measures among these groups.

- **Harm reduction program for IDUs.** Injection use appears to be a growing problem in MENA, which raises the risk of HIV spread. Yet, access to harm reduction programs is almost nonexistent in the region. Less than 1 percent of the IDU group has access to such activities.

- **Behavioral interventions.** Only 5 percent of sex workers and their clients, 10 percent of MSMs, 2 percent of out-of-school youth, and 27 percent of in-school youth have access to behavioral interventions.

- **Diagnosis and treatment of STDs.** Only about 16 percent of the population who need STD treatment is able to obtain it.

- **Voluntary counseling and testing (VCT).** Compared with other regions, MENA countries have the largest coverage gap with only 6 percent of the target group having access to VCT.

- **HIV/AIDS awareness.** For a variety of reasons (lack of political response and so on) there is a general lack of HIV awareness. Most people believe that they are not at risk of infection. In total, less than 20 percent of the people at risk of infection have access to HIV/AIDS information.

Benefits of interventions

Substantial benefits would arise from the implementation of the intervention measures. In addition to these monetary gains there would also be additional welfare gains. In total, the population would benefit as follows:

- First, at the macroeconomic level, the projected loss of GDP output would be substantially reduced (Table A1.2), which would increase per capita income. Given the strong impact of GDP growth on poverty, the number of poor people would be much less than in the absence of preventive measures. In aggregate, between 8 and 30 million people

FIGURE A1.6

Percent of Individuals at Risk with Access to Interventions

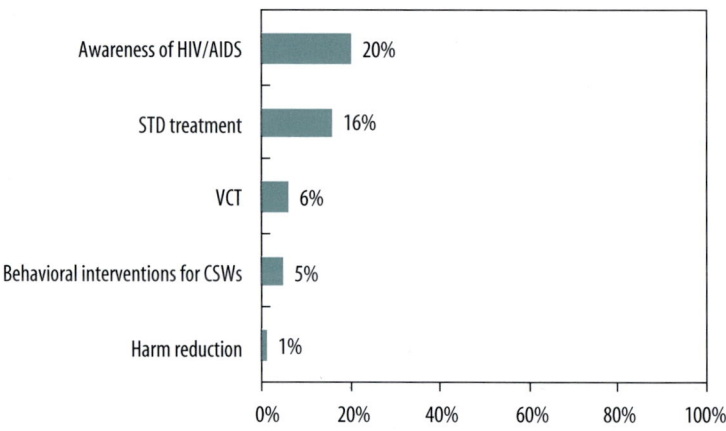

Source: Global HIV Prevention Working Group. 2003. "Access to HIV Prevention: Closing the Gap." Convened by the Bill and Melinda Gates Foundation and the Henry J. Kaiser Family Foundation.

Note: CSW, commercial sex workers; STD, sexually transmitted disease; VCT, voluntary counseling and testing.

could escape poverty depending on how sensitive poverty prevalence is to economic growth (Jenkins and Robalino 2003).

- Second, the population at large will benefit directly from avoidance of HIV infection. New infections would be reduced, especially among young people and women. Over time, the reduction in infections would lead to less suffering and premature deaths.

- Third, these interventions would help improve standards of living among disadvantaged groups and reduce income inequality. People living with HIV/AIDS, CSWs, MSM, IDUs, and people in correctional institutions will be able to better protect themselves, and benefit from reduced stigma and improved human rights.

- Fourth, the early implementation of interventions will reduce the future number of HIV/AIDS patients and orphans. As a result, the costs of treatment and care of HIV/AIDS patients would be reduced. This will allow countries to allocate the savings to productive investments and significantly improve long-term per capita income growth.

Cost effectiveness of interventions

International experience has demonstrated that prevention interventions to reduce the spread of HIV/AIDS are cost effective, especially when focused on reducing risks in those groups most likely to contact and spread HIV/AIDS. Interventions such as provision of basic prevention packages for high-risk and vulnerable groups, as well as harm reduction for IDUs, have proven highly effective.[14]

Additional evidence is also available in the case of MENA countries. Expanding condom use by 30 percent and access to safe needles for IDUs by 20 percent was found to have substantial benefits for the period 2000–25. Among MENA countries, the net gains (that is, after subtracting the cost of interventions) would range from 17 to 40 percent of today's GDP (figure A1.7). On average this translates into an increase of 0.3 percent in GDP growth rate.

However, the benefits decline sharply if these interventions are delayed. As an example, delaying the interventions by five years can cost countries an average of 8 percent of today's GDP (27 percent in the case of Djibouti) (figure A1.8). Put differently, inaction can make more than half of the economic decline unavoidable for most MENA countries. Historic evidence corroborates the benefits of acting early. For example, the efforts of Senegal to act early have certainly contributed to keeping the HIV prevalence rate at a low level. Thailand's program is another example that illustrates the benefits of early action.

FIGURE A1.7

Net Benefits from Increasing Access to Condoms and Safe Needles for IDUs in 2000–25

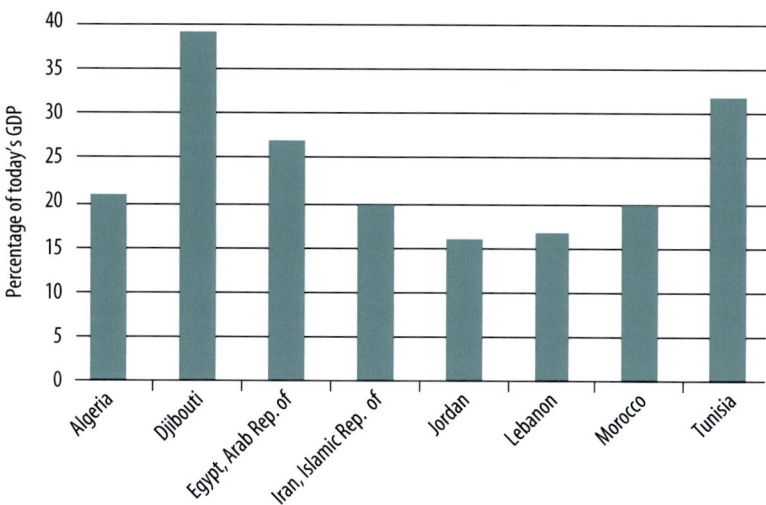

Source: Jenkins, C., and David A. Robalino. 2003. *HIV/AIDS in the Middle East and North Africa: The Costs of Inaction.* World Bank.

FIGURE A1.8

Losses Incurred by Delaying Interventions by Five Years in 2000–25

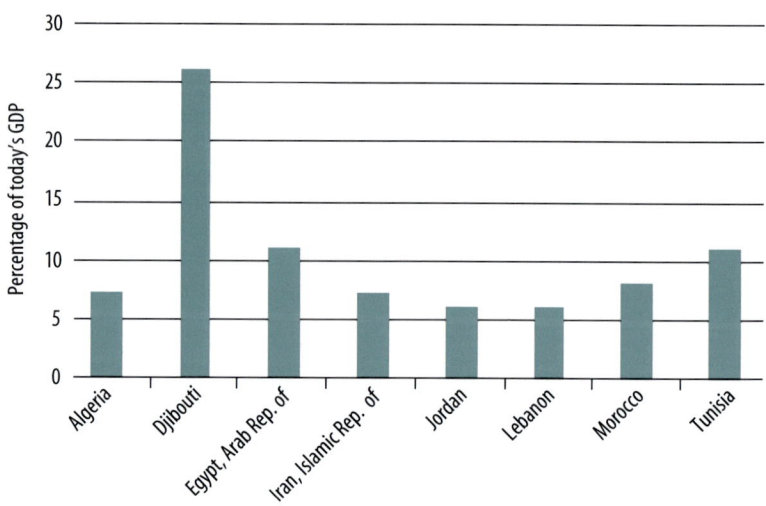

Source: Jenkins, C., and David A. Robalino. 2003. *HIV/AIDS in the Middle East and North Africa: The Costs of Inaction.* World Bank.

Notes

1. Approximately 5.1 million people were estimated to be HIV positive at end-2003.
2. For example, cholera epidemics may last for only a few months in any one location.
3. In the case of most other infectious diseases, the rapid onset of illness and diseases has the benefit of alerting public officials early on. This happened most recently with the Ebola fever. Faced with increased mortality, countries took measures to control the spread of the disease and to immobilize the victims of the disease, thereby reducing their potential to infect other individuals. As a result, the socioeconomic effects of the Ebola fever were limited to the short term.
4. Bell, C., S. Devarajan, and H. Gersbach, The Long-Run Economic Costs of AIDS: Theory and Application to South Africa, Policy Research Working Paper No. 3152 (World Bank, 2003).
5. Bell, C., H. Gersbach, R. Bruhns, and D. Völker, "Economic Growth, Human Capital and Population in Kenya in the Time of AIDS: A Long-Run Analysis in Historical Perspective" (draft, August 2004).
6. Currently, they are estimated to amount to 1 to 6 percent of the wage bill for South African firms, but they are projected to rise to 15 percent of the wage bill by 2015 (Metropolitan Insurance).
7. Jenkins, C., and David A. Robalino, "HIV/AIDS in the Middle East and North Africa: The Costs of Inaction" (World Bank, 2003).
8. Haacker, M., "Modeling the Macroeconomic Impact of HIV/AIDS" (IMF Working Paper, WP/2/195, 2002).
9. Those countries had female school enrollment rates below 40 percent in 1990–95, which created a significant risk of vulnerability.
10. See the reference in note 6 for more details on the econometric model that was used to account for the level of HIV prevalence rates in MENA countries.
11. The model predicts the international variations in HIV/AIDS prevalence levels as a function of: income per capita, female participation in labor force, female literacy, the Gini index of inequality, the share of tourism-related activities in gross domestic product (GDP), and migration.
12. Same reference as in note 6.
13. These impacts are estimated by averaging the outcomes of the various scenarios.
14. See, for example, Commission on Macroeconomics and Health, "The Evidence Base for Interventions to prevent HIV infection in Low- and Middle-Income Countries" (Paper No. WG5: 2, 2001).

Reported AIDS Cases in the MENA Region, 1990 to Mid-2003

Country	1990	1991	1992	1993	1994	1995	1996	1997	1998	1999	2000	2001	2002	Mid-2003[a]	Total	Population ('000s)	Rate per 100,00
Algeria	27	35	34	31	53	32	48	39	49	24	58	17	—	—	501	30,841	1
Bahrain	2	—	6	3	6	10	11	14	11	9	8	7	17	2	108	652	16
Djibouti	51	107	144	144	196	231	358	434	111	267	131	—	—	—	2,181	644	33
Egypt, Arab Rep. of	7	12	23	29	22	16	14	25	33	34	44	42	47	21	389	69,080	0
Iran, Islamic Rep. of	10	25	16	32	19	16	27	40	21	27	68	76	271	43	700	71,369	1
Iraq	—	7	6	21	37	16	15	2	4	6	6	4	—	—	124	23,584	0
Israel	38	28	46	47	32	45	67	45	36	137	50	39	78	22	807	6,172	13
Jordan	1	8	7	8	6	2	4	12	11	3	14	10	11	2	111	5,051	2
Kuwait	1	3	2	2	5	4	5	2	19	4	12	10	5	3	79	1,971	4
Lebanon	10	13	7	22	12	18	5	8	37	32	21	21	43	4	265	3,556	7
Libya[b]	11	6	9	2	11	16	21	38	396	72	—	—	—	—	611	5,471	11
Morocco	26	28	30	44	77	57	66	92	93	165	118	129	150	39	1158	30,430	3
Oman	22	25	32	37	51	28	24	36	33	45	30	35	48	15	530	2,622	20
Qatar	10	13	5	8	8	6	2	4	3	9	10	3	6	—	139	575	24
Saudi Arabia[c]	5	10	6	12	38	37	100	112	39	24	24	29	—	—	465	21,028	2
Syrian Arab Rep.	1	7	3	3	4	6	9	8	8	7	7	14	13	2	104	16,61	0
Tunisia	36	36	38	52	50	65	54	62	44	42	44	48	36	10	676	9,562	8
United Arab Emirates	8	1	3	1	2	1	2	1	1	2	—	—	—	—	22	2,398	0
West Bank and Gaza[d]	0	1	8	2	7	5	1	8	3	4	4	5	0	—	39 AIDS / 14 HIV	3.306	1 / AID
Yemen, Republic of	1	0	3	4	3	11	60	40	34	34	18	31	16	—	255	19,114	1

Sources: UNAIDS/WHO: EMRO statistics for all but Oman; Oman's updated statistics were offered by Geneva/WHO; Palestine: Joudah, Izzat., NAP Manage STD-HIV/AIDS Epidemiology Palestine www.emro.who.int/asd/Presentations/Palestine%20STD%20HIV%20AIDS.ppt, accessed December 22, 2003; Isra UNAIDS Update 2002; European Centre for Epidemiological Monitoring of AIDS, Report No 69, 2003.

Note:— Not available.

a. January 1 through June 3, 2002.

b. The Libyan daily *ash-Shams* quoted national AIDS program Director Ahmad Mahmoud as saying that about 800 Libyan patients and 175 foreign reside in the country have AIDS (UPI, December 27, 2003).

c. *Al Jazeera* (October 23, 2003) reported that the Ministry of Health announced that it had registered 1,509 Saudi nationals as AIDS patients.

d. Figures include both HIV and AIDS.

Profiles of the HIV/AIDS Epidemics in Countries of the MENA Region

Country	Date of First Recorded AIDS Case	Estimated Adult Prevalence Level (Percent)(UNAIDS/WHO)	Estimated Adults and Children Living with HIV/AIDS (Reported [r] and Estimate [e] by UNAIDS/WHO, End 2001)ᵃ	Female Reported AIDS Cases or Reported HIV Infections (Percent)	HIV in High-Risk Groups (Percent)	Features of Epidemic Transmission Modes among Reported AIDS Cases, 1997–2001; HIV Prevalence in General Population; Major Risks; Indicators of Change
Algeria	1985	0.1	1,067 (1/01) [r]; 13,000 (adults) [e]	27 (AIDS, 2001)	1.2 in FSWs (1988); 0.10 in 20 FSWs (2000); 3 in 139 FSWs (2000); STD clinics at 6 sites, 9 (2/22) at Tamanrasset, 1.7 (2/117) at Oran, rest zero (2000).	41% heterosexual, 5% homosexual, 18% IDU, 10% blood, 2% MTCT, <1% other, and 24% unknown; 0.9% HIV prevalence at 4 antenatal sites (2000); 0.3% in 345 TB patients (1998); 0.4 in 1,984 antenatal mothers (2000); high levels of migrants from West and Central Africa transiting through southern area; FSWs from Algeria and elsewhere.
Bahrain	1985	0.3	216 (December 2000 [r]); <1,000 [e]	7 (AIDS, 2001); 11 (HIV, July 2001)	1.6 in 242 multitransfused children with hemolytic anemias (1995); 0.3 in 291 IDUs (2000); 0.9–2.3 in IDUs (1998).	11% heterosexual, 4% homosexual/bisexual, 72% IDU, 2.4% MTCT, and 10% blood; 67% all cases in IDUs (2001); 0 in 2,079 blood donors (1999); 0.2 in 627 antenatal women (1998); migrant sex trade, opiates.
Djibouti	1986	2.9 (1.1–4.7, 95% CI, 2002)	3,500–14,500 [e] (1999)	21 (AIDS, 1997–98); 54 among 15- to 29-year-old cohort.	22 in STD patients (1996); 28 in FSWs (1998); >50 in street sex workers and 26 in bar sex workers (1996).	99% heterosexual and 1% MTCT (1997–98); 1.9% in private antenatal clinic (1999); 26% in TB patients (2001); 1.8%–3.1% in blood donors (2000); STDs: 3.2% syphilis in antenatal mothers (1997); in 2002, general population 2.8% (95% CI 1.2% to 4.5%, 1999); high levels of commercial sex; 100,000 refugees sent home; 5,000–10,000 resettled in camps (2003).
Egypt, Arab Rep. of	1986	<0.1	1,711 (1,153 Egyptians, 558 foreigners; 368 with AIDS, May 2003) [r]; 8,000 [e]	11; 17.3 (NAP, end-2001); 19% (HIV, end-2001)	1 in 102 MSM (1999); 0.79 in 382 MSM (2000); 0.86 in 815 MSM (2001); 0 in 129 FSW (2001); 0 in 920 STD patients (2001).	54% heterosexual, 11% homosexual, 24% blood, <1% MTCT, and 9% unknown (end 2001); 0.006% in blood donors (2001); 0 antenatal; 0.6% in TB patients; 75% infections acquired in Egypt; 16% drug users are IDUs , 31% of whom share equipment (2001); 4,897 drug users tested

ANNEX 3, *continued*

Country	Date of First Recorded AIDS Case	Estimated Adult Prevalence Level (Percent)(UNAIDS/WHO)	Estimated Adults and Children Living with HIV/AIDS (Reported [r] and Estimate [e] by UNAIDS/WHO, End 2001)*	Female Reported AIDS Cases or Reported HIV Infections (Percent)	HIV in High-Risk Groups (Percent)	Features of Epidemic Transmission Mode among Reported AIDS Cases, 1997–2001; HIV Prevalence in General Population; Major Risks; Indicators of Change
Egypt, Arab Rep. of						between 1986/2001, 0.2%; small samples in early to mid-1990s in Cairo and Alexandria drug users up to 7.6%; threat of HIV transmission among IDU seems significant.
Iran, Islamic Rep. of	1986	<0.1	626 AIDS [r] October 2002; 20,000 [e]	5.1 (end 2002)	0.72 in 140,277 drug users tested over time; 0.5 in 8,202 IDUs (1998); 2.3% among prisoners, mostly drug users, in 2000; 0 in 5,700 STD patients (1998); 0 in 1,605 FSWs (1998).	15.8% sexual; 52.7% IDU, 19.8% blood, 0.3% MTCT, and 11.3% unknown (2002); 4.2% in TB patients (2002); rapid threefold increase in HIV/AIDS in 2001–02; 4% among VCT center users (2001); sex work, polygamy also risk factors; estimated 30,000 CSWs (2002); 170,000 IDUs; estimated that prevalence remains around 15% among IDUs and <5% among FSWs.
Iraq	1986	<0.1	180 as of April 2003 [r]; <1,000 [e]	9	Mandatory screening for prisoners, STD patients, health and hotel workers; premarital tests, etc.	9.3% heterosexual, 86.1% blood, and 4.6% MTCT (1999); STDs: reported cases increased between 1999 and 2000; 0.1% syphilis and 0 HIV in pregnant women (2000); war zone, sex work.
Israel	1983	0.1 (end-2001)	2,700 [e]	22% (end-2001)	STD patients-immigrant workers, n=900, 0.6 (2002).	46.8% heterosexual, 24.8% homosexual, 13.2% IDU, and 2.9% MTCT (mid-2003); cumulative HIV detected, 3,802 (mid-2003); between 1999 and mid-2003: 54.3% heterosexual, 14.4% homosexual, 13.2% IDU, 2.7% MTCT; transmission among homosexuals appears to be decreasing, IDU levels about the same as earlier; large Eastern European migrant sex trade, HIV levels unknown.

Country	Year	Prevalence (%)	Reported [r] / Estimated [e] cases	AIDS / HIV cases	Surveillance	Epidemiology
Jordan	1986	<0.1	324 cumulative, 131 (40%) Jordanians as of June 2003 [r]; <1,000 [e]	13 (AIDS); 26 (HIV/AIDS) (NAP, 2003)	No surveillance except prisoners; none infected of 945 tested (2000).	40% heterosexual, 3.2% homosexual, 3.2% IDU, 38.9% blood (1997–00), 1.1% MTCT, and 13.7% unknown; only 1 of 281 TB patients infected; 0.03% among blood donors; none among antenatal mothers tested 1992, 1994, 1999; KAP study (1999) of 3,200 people revealed 4%–16% sex outside of marriage in last year, of which 10% MSM; small study of 56 FSWs, 3–5 clients/day; 25% condom use (2003).
Kuwait (includes expatriates)	1984	0.12	835 (December 2000) [r]; 1,300 [e]	18 HIV/Aids	0 in 2,600 STD patients; mandatory testing for sexual offense prisoners, IDUs in treatment/ custody; 0 in 193 IDUs (2000).	73% heterosexual, 6% homosexual, 6% IDUs; 2% MTCT; 6% blood, and 8% unknown; 275,307 people screened in 2000,1.7% HIV positive; 0 in pregnant women; STDs: increased from 1,002 in 1991 to 6,043 in 1997; 30% gonorrhea, 1.6% syphilis; HIV types B & C, via India; migrants/sex/heroin.
Lebanon	1984	0.09	700 (October 2003) [r]; 1,500 [e]	16 (AIDS); 21 (HIV/AIDS, December 1999)	In 1999, 0 infected of 205 select FSWs; 0.2 in prisoners; 6.3% of all reported HIV cases are IDUs, all males.	47% heterosexual, 28% homosexual, 3% IDUs, 15.6% blood,and 6.7% MTCT (cumulative); >50% recent cases local origin; rising percentageof women; general population behavioral surveys in 1991 and 1996 show drop in use of condom from 40% to 33%; NSP reports 68% of 15–24 year olds sexually active, 33% with multiple partners, 76% never used condoms; 33% IDUs had commercial sex in last month.
Libya	1990	0.2	800 +175 foreigners (December 2003) [r]; 7,000 [e]	—	571 new infections in 2000, 98% among IDUs; 319 in 2001.	56% heterosexual, 22% blood, and 22% MTCT (cumulative), but not currently accurate; outbreaks in hospitals from lack of infection control, 370 children in 1998; 0.3% in 296 TB patients (1998).
Morocco (includes expatriates)	1986	0.1	963 (94% Moroccan, December 2001) [r]; 12,000–15,000 [e]	36 AIDS; 50 HIV (among new cases)	0.1 in 7402 STD patients (2001); 2.3% in CSWs (2001).	70% heterosexual, 9% homosexual, 6% IDUs, 3% blood, 2% MTCT, 6% other, and 4% unknown; <1% in antenatal women (2001); rising rates in some areas, Tangiers higher in IDUs, Marrakech higher in MSM.

ANNEX 3, *continued*

Country	Date of First Recorded AIDS Case	Estimated Adult Prevalence Level (Percent)(UNAIDS/WHO)	Estimated Adults and Children Living with HIV/AIDS (Reported [r] and Estimate [e] by UNAIDS/WHO, End 2001)[a]	Female Reported AIDS Cases or Reported HIV Infections (Percent)	HIV in High-Risk Groups (Percent)	Features of Epidemic Transmission Mode among Reported AIDS Cases, 1997–2001; HIV Prevalence in General Population; Major Risks; Indicators of Change
Oman	1987	0.1	833 (November 2003) [r]; 1,300 [e]	32 HIV/AIDS	In 1999, 5 in 135 arrested IDUs; 8.3 among 60 IDUs	41% heterosexual, 11% homosexual, 2% IDUs, 22% blood, 6% MTCT, 2% other, and (2000); 0 HIV in 337 STD patients (2001). 17% unknown; 2% in TB patients (2000); STDs: incidence rate of reported cases dropped from 92 to 48.6 per 100,000 between 1996 and 2000; among 245 men in social clubs, 13% nonmarital sex in past year (1995).
Qatar	—	0.09	300 [e]	29 (cumulative AIDS)	In 1999, 5 in 2,249 STD patients.	20% heterosexual, 4.8% homosexual, 58% blood, 8% MTCT, and 9.6% unknown; 0 in 2,464 blood donors (1999).
Saudi Arabia	1984	—	~6,787 [r, cumulative, 23/10/03]; 22% Saudi nationals	20 (AIDS, 2003)	2.3 in multitransfused children (1989); 0.14 in 2,102 IDUs (1997).	72% heterosexual, 6% homosexual, 2% IDUs, 15% blood, and 4% MTCT (1997–98); 8/10/02-report of 452 AIDS, additional 833 HIV=1,285 HIV/AIDS; 436 cumulative by 2000; 350 cases reported 2001, 200 in 2002, rose to 800 in 2003; 450 died (as of 9/03); rise due to suspected improvement in reporting.
Syrian Arab Rep.	1987	0.01	145 (July 1999) [r]; 800 [e]	19 (NAP, 2001)	As of 1998, STD patients 0.12; FSWs 0.12; bar girls 0.04; MSM 0.59; 0 in IDUs.	73% heterosexual, 8% homosexual, 8% blood, and 4% MTCT (1997–2000); 250,000 people tested yearly, almost all mandatory; 0.0015% in blood donors, 0.005% in Syrian travelers before departure; few cases detected; STDs: April–June 1999, 2,342 cases reported at four centers according to syndromic method.
Tunisia (includes expatriates)	1985	0.06 (March 2001)	1,125, 738 alive (December 2002) [r]; 2,200 [e]	40 (AIDS, 1998–99)	0 to <1 in registered FSWs throughout 1990s; 0 in 570 FSWs (1999), 0.22 in 458 FSWs (2001).	51% heterosexual, 10% homosexual, 27% IDUs, 8% blood, 4% MTCT (1998–99); 0 in 108 antenatal mothers (1999); >50% detected as AIDS; all infected females and30% males acquired infection in Tunisia; high proportion among expatriates; 0.25% in TB patients (1996); 0.003% in blood donors; by 2002, all new HIV cases among women through sexual transmission; among males 10% IDU, 6% heterosexual, 3% homosexual.

United Arab Emirates	—	0.18	2,300 (January 2000) [e]	—	—	—	54.7% heterosexual, 18.9% blood, 5.7% homosexual/bisexual; 3.8% IDU, 1.9% MTCT, and 15% unknown (HIV/AIDS, 2002).
West Bank and Gaza	1988	1.6	72 (December 2003) [r]	19 AIDS	—	—	—
Yemen, Republic of	1990	0.01 (1999)	1,077 (June 2002) [r]; 6,400–13,000 [e]	33 (2000); approx.	50 HIV (2000)	5 in 88 FSWs (1998); 3 in 585 STD patients (1998); 27 in 147 prisoners (1998); 2.7 in FSWs (1999); 7 in FSWs, (2001); 1.8 in 284 STD patients (2000).	77.3% heterosexual, 15.9% homosexual, and 6.8% blood (1998); more than 50% infections acquired in Yemen; gender ratio changed from 4:1 (male to female) in 1995 to 2:1 in 1999 and 1:1 in 2000; 0.7% in 11,070 low-risk people (1998); 0.04% in 19,813 blood donors (1998) rose to 0.28% in 2000; 6.9% in TB patients (1999); 45% HIV infections among Yemenis.

— Not available.

Note: CI, confidence interval; FSW, female sex worker; IDU, injecting drug user; KAP, knowledge, attitude, practice; MTCT, mother-to-child transmission; MSM, men who have sex with men; NAP, National AIDS Program; STD, sexually transmitted disease; TB, tuberculosis; VCT, voluntary counseling and testing.

a. Unless otherwise indicated.

References for Annex 3

Abdelmajid, B.H. 1999. Situation épidémiologique des maladies sexuellement transmissibles. Chapitre 1 in *Les 7èmes* (JNSP/DSSB/99). Department of Preventive Medicine, Faculty of Medicine, Tunis. Mimeo.

Agence France Press. 2002. "Saudi Arabia Reports 1,285 HIV/AIDS Cases." October 8.

Al-Jowder, S. 2001. "Bahrain Report." Prepared for the WHO 11th Intercountry Meeting of National AIDS and STD Program Managers, Casablanca, July.

Al-Owaish, R.A., S. Anwar, P. Sharma, and S.F. Shah. 2000. "HIV/AIDS Prevalence among Male Patients in Kuwait." *Saudi Medical Journal* 21(9):852–59.

As'ad, A., and R. Al-Azzeh. 2001. "Jordan Country Report." Prepared for the WHO 11th Intercountry Meeting of National AIDS and STD Program Managers, Casablanca, July.

Bakaric, S. 2003. "AIDS Patients Twice Stricken under Saddam Hussein." *Agence France Presse*, April 5.

Ba-Omer, A.A. 2001. "HIV/AIDS/STD Situation and Management in Oman." Prepared for the WHO 11th Intercountry Meeting of National AIDS and STD Program Managers, Casablanca, July.

Ben Said, A. 2001. "National AIDS and STDs Program in Tunisia." Prepared for the WHO 11th Intercountry Meeting of National AIDS and STD Program Managers, Casablanca, July.

———. 2002. Point sur la situation épidémiologique de l'infection a VIH/SIDA en Tunisie. Mimeo.

Bouakaz, R. Juillet. 1998. Ministère de la Santé et de la Population, Direction de la Prévention Institut National de Santé Publique. Santé Sud. Mimeo.

———. 2000. Migration et SIDA au Sud Algérien: Cas de Tamanrasset. La Wilaye de Tamanrasset. Mimeo.

Dareini, A.A. 2002. "Rise in Iranian Prostitution Blamed on Strict Sex Rules, Economy." Associated Press, September 15.

Elharti, E., S. Nadia, B. Ouafae, M. Rajae, S. Amina, and E.A. Rajae. 2002. "HIV Epidemiology in Morocco: A Nine-Year Survey (1991–1999)." *International Journal of STD and AIDS* 13:839–42.

Egyptian National AIDS Program. 2001. "HIV/AIDS Surveillance in Egypt." Prepared for the WHO 11th Intercountry Meeting of National AIDS and STD Program Managers, Casablanca, July.

El Nakib, M. 2001. "HIV/AIDS Lebanon Country Report." Prepared for WHO 11th Intercountry Meeting of National AIDS and STD Program Managers, Casablanca, July.

El-Sayed, N. 2002. Egypt Ministry of Health and Population, National AIDS Control Program. PowerPoint presentation entitled "First Consultation of the Regional Advisory Panel on the Impact of Drug Abuse" (RAPID) at the WHO/EMRO meeting held in Cairo, Egypt, September 23–26.

El-Sayed, N., P. Gomatos, C. Beck-Sagué, U. Dietrich, H. von Briesen, S. Osmanov, J. Esparza, R. Arthur, M. Wahdan, and W. Jarvis. 2000. "Epidemic Transmission of Human Immunodeficiency Virus in Renal Dialysis Centers." *The Arab Republic of Egypt. Journal of Infectious Diseases* 181:91–97.

Etchepare, M. 2001. Programme National de Lutte Contre le SIDA et les MST, Draft report prepared for the World Bank Mission for Health Project Strategy Development, p. 47.

———. March 2002. Enquête nationale séroprévalence VIH en République de Djibouti, Report Summary. Washington, DC: World Bank. Mimeo.

EuroHIV. 2003. HIV/AIDS Surveillance in Europe. End-year report 2003, No. 69, December 2003. European Centre for Epidemiological Monitoring of AIDS; WHO and UNAIDS Collaborating Centre on AIDS.

Family Health International (FHI). 2001. HIV/AIDS/STI Prevention Program Support Strategy for Jordan. Mimeo.

Farza, A.M. 2001. Rapport de Fin de Mission D'Assistance Technique pour la Formulation du Plan Stratégique National de Lutte Control de SIDA, 2002-2004 au Maroc, Rabat, Mars-Juin. Mimeo.

Garbouj, M. 2003. 'Le point sur l'épidémie du VIH/SIDA en Tunisie Strategies et Perspectives.' PowerPoint presentation. Mimeo.

GFATM Proposal, Algeria. 2003.

GFATM Proposal, Iran. 2003.

GFATM Proposal, Jordan. 2003.

GFATM Proposal, Morocco. 2003.

GFATM Proposal, Yemen. 2003.

Hassan, J. 2003. "Saudi Women Make Up 20% of AIDS Cases." *Arab News, Saudi Arabia*, September 3.

Hermez, J. 2002. "Experiences in Research, Outreach and the Role of NGOs. Lebanese National AIDS Control Programme." PowerPoint presentation at WHO/EMRO meeting entitled "First Consultation of the Regional Advisory Panel on the Impact of Drug Abuse (RAPID)," Cairo, September 23–26.

Islamic Republic of Iran. 2001 "AIDS in Islamic Republic of Iran." Prepared for the WHO 11th Intercountry Meeting of National AIDS and STD Program Managers, Casablanca, July.

Joudah, I. 2003. "STD-HIV/AIDS Epidemiology Palestine." PowerPoint presentation, May.

Kassak, K. May 2003. Draft. Situational Analysis and Response Review-Lebanon. Mimeo.

Kuwait National AIDS Program. 2001. "Progress Report of National AIDS Program, State of Kuwait, 2001." Prepared for WHO 11th Intercountry Meeting of National AIDS and STD Program Managers, Casablanca, July.

Ministry of Health (Djibouti). 2001. *HIV/AIDS Epidemic and Sexually Transmitted Diseases in Djibouti Republic.* Djibouti, July 23.

Ministry of Health (Jordan) in collaboration with UNAIDS and WHO. 1999. *Knowledge, Attitudes, Beliefs and Practices on AIDS in Jordan.* Jordan.

Ministry of Health and Population (Egypt). 2001. "National AIDS Control Program, the Arab Republic of Egypt." In *HIV/AIDS Prevention and Control*, p. 7. Mimeo.

Ministry of Public Health (Tunisia). 2000. *Summary Report for International Forum on the Implementation of the ICPD Program of Action, 1994-1999.* Tunis: National Family and Population Board.

———. 2001. *Atelier national de concertation sur la lutte contre le VIH/SIDA en Tunisie.* Tunis, Mars 30. Mimeo.

Morocco National AIDS Program. 2001. "Country Report." Prepared for the WHO 11th Intercountry Meeting of National AIDS and STD Program Managers, Casablanca, July.

Mosbah, F., and C. Yahi. 1998. Prévention de la Toxicomanie et Santé Sexuelle et Reproductive. Enquête Qualitative sur les Jeunes. Association Tunisienne du Planning Familial.

National AIDS Program, Iran. 2001. "AIDS in Islamic Republic of Iran." Prepared for the WHO 11th Intercountry Meeting of National AIDS and STD Program Managers, Casablanca, July.

Njoh, J., and S. Zimmo. 1997. "The Prevalence of Human Immunodeficiency Virus among Drug-Dependent Patients in Jeddah, Saudi Arabia." *Journal of Substance Abuse and Treatment*, 14(5):487–8.

Oman Daily Observer. 2003. "Sultanate Steps Up Efforts to Combat AIDS." December 9.

Preble, E. (AIDSCAP). 1996. "Needs Assessment for HIV/AIDS Control and Prevention in the Arab Republic of Egypt." A Report to the U.S. Agency for International Development, Cairo, Egypt, June. Mimeo.

République Algérienne Démocratique et Populaire Ministère de la Santé et de la Population/Direction de la Prévention/Institut National de Santé Publique. 2000. 'Surveillance des Risques de Santé Liés à la Route Transsaharienne.' Premier séminaire d'information et d'évaluation du projet PNUD/Gouvernement ALG/94/010, Mars. Mimeo.

Reuters News Service. 2000. "Oman Says Has 600 AIDS Cases, 70 Percent Are Men." April 12.

———. 2001. "Bahrain Visa Curbs Only on Women from CIS States." May 1.

Rosa, B. 1999. "Serosurveillance Epidémiologique de L'Infection au VIH par Réseau Sentinelle." These de DESM, Université D'Alger, Faculté de Médecine D'Alger, Dept. of Médecine.

Sow, A. 2001. "HIV/AIDS Epidemic and Sexually Transmitted Diseases in Dji-bouti Republic." Prepared for the WHO 11th Intercountry Meeting of National AIDS and STD Program Managers, Casablanca, July.

Spratt, K. February 2000. HIV/AIDS and Sexually Transmitted Infections (STIs) in the West Bank and Gaza. USAID.

Syrian Arab Republic. 2001. "Country Report." Prepared for the WHO 11th Intercountry Meeting of National AIDS and STD Program Managers, Casablanca, July.

Tawilah, J. 2001. "HIV/AIDS Epidemic in the EMR." PowerPoint presentation, October.

Tchupo, J.P. February 1998. 'Les maladies sexuellement transmissibles en République de Djibouti: Evaluation de la situation et recommandations pour une prise en charge optimale.' Rapport de Mission. UNAIDS. Mimeo.

UNAIDS Expanded Theme Group on HIV/AIDS in Egypt. 2003. Assessment of the HIV/AIDS Situation and Response in Egypt. May.

UNAIDS/WHO. 2002a. AIDS Epidemic Update. December 2002. Geneva: UNAIDS/WHO.

———. 2002b. Algeria Epidemiological Fact Sheet on HIV/AIDS and Sexually Transmitted Infections. 2002 Update. Geneva, UNAIDS/WHO.

———. 2002c. Bahrain Epidemiological Fact Sheet on HIV/AIDS and Sexually Transmitted Infections. 2002 Update. Geneva, UNAIDS/WHO.

———. 2002d. Djibouti Epidemiological Fact Sheet on HIV/AIDS and Sexually Transmitted Infections. 2002 Update. Geneva, UNAIDS/WHO.

———. 2002e. Egypt Epidemiological Fact Sheet on HIV/AIDS and Sexually Transmitted Infections. 2002 Update. Geneva: UNAIDS/WHO.

———. 2002f. Islamic Republic of Iran Epidemiological Fact Sheet on HIV/AIDS and Sexually Transmitted Infections. 2002 Update. Geneva, UNAIDS/WHO.

———. 2002g. Jordan Epidemiological Fact Sheet on HIV/AIDS and Sexually Transmitted Infections. 2002 Update. Geneva, UNAIDS/WHO.

———. 2002h. Kuwait Epidemiological Fact Sheet on HIV/AIDS and Sexually Transmitted Infections. 2002 Update. Geneva, UNAIDS/WHO.

———. 2002i. Lebanon Epidemiological Fact Sheet on HIV/AIDS and Sexually Transmitted Infections. 2002 Update. Geneva, UNAIDS/WHO.

———. 2002j. Libya Epidemiological Fact Sheet on HIV/AIDS and Sexually Transmitted Infections. 2002 Update. Geneva, UNAIDS/WHO.

———. 2002k. Morocco Epidemiological Fact Sheet on HIV/AIDS and Sexually Transmitted Infections. 2002 Update. Geneva, UNAIDS/WHO.

———. 2002l. Oman Epidemiological Fact Sheet on HIV/AIDS and Sexually Transmitted Infections. 2002 Update. Geneva, UNAIDS/WHO.

———. 2002m. Qatar Epidemiological Fact Sheet on HIV/AIDS and Sexually Transmitted Infections. 2002 Update. Geneva, UNAIDS/WHO.

———. 2002n. Saudi Arabia Epidemiological Fact Sheet on HIV/AIDS and Sexually Transmitted Infections. 2002 Update. Geneva, UNAIDS/WHO.

————. 2002o. Syria Epidemiological Fact Sheet on HIV/AIDS and Sexually Transmitted Infections. 2002 Update. Geneva, UNAIDS/WHO.

————. 2002p. Tunisia Epidemiological Fact Sheet on HIV/AIDS and Sexually Transmitted Infections. 2002 Update. Geneva, UNAIDS/WHO.

————. 2002q. United Arab Emirates Epidemiological Fact Sheet on HIV/AIDS and Sexually Transmitted Infections. 2002 Update. Geneva, UNAIDS/WHO.

————. 2002r. Yemen Epidemiological Fact Sheet on HIV/AIDS and Sexually Transmitted Infections. 2002 Update. Geneva:, UNAIDS/WHO.

United Nations Development Programme (UNDP), Office of Palestinian Territories. 2004. "Moving Beyond Denial-Breaking the Silence around HIV-AIDS in Palestine." UNDP-PAPP Position Paper on HIV-AIDS.

United Press International. 2003. "Libya Registers 975 AIDS Cases." December 27.

World Health Organization/Eastern Mediterranean Regional Office (WHO/EMRO). 1995. "Report on the Intercountry Workshop on Evaluation of National AIDS Programs" (WHO-EM/GPA/111/E). Nicosia, Cyprus, August 22–25. Mimeo.

————. 2000. "Regional Consultation on Reducing Risk of and Vulnerability to HIV/AIDS in Countries of the Eastern Mediterranean Region." Tunis, Tunisia, May 29–June 1.

————. 2003. Division of Communicable Disease Control. Annual Report 2002. WHO/EM/DCD/003/E/G.

Details of National Strategic Plans on HIV/AIDS in MENA, January 2004

Algeria has finalized her multisectoral National Strategic Plan (NSP) for HIV/AIDS for the period of 2003–06, in collaboration with nongovernmental organizations (NGOs) and international partners. The government has been approved to receive $8.8 million designated for the next two years from the Global Fund to Fight HIV/AIDS, Tuberculosis and Malaria (GFATM) to implement its multisectoral Action Plan to fight HIV/AIDS, with the participation of communities and the civil society. Additionally, for a number of years, an association of people living with HIV/AIDS (PLWHA) has been established and a network of NGOs working on HIV/AIDS is now in place. Specific preventive activities have been supported among religious leaders, prisons, and police forces. Currently, plans are proceeding to strengthen surveillance and to undertake a study on drug use and HIV/AIDS.

The increased political level of commitment to fight HIV/AIDS is apparent in the president's speech on December 1, 2003, to commemorate the World AIDS Day in Algeria (see box A4.1 below).

Djibouti has the most advanced epidemic among MENA countries (2.9% among adults). With the help of the Bank, it has developed a multisectoral strategy and has obtained a $12 million International Development Association (IDA) grant to implement a joint HIV/AIDS, tuberculosis, and malaria strategic plan. In addition, the International Road Corridor Rehabilitation in Djibouti is a Bank-funded project (loan) that has an HIV/AIDS component aimed at diminishing the potential for increased transmission of HIV in the trucking industry and at construction sites. Djibouti is also one of the six countries of the Horn of Africa that are benefiting from an Institutional Development Grant from the Bank to their Inter-Governmental Authority on Development. The grant mainly focuses on building the HIV/AIDS monitoring and evaluation (M&E) capacity of member states. The French government had been funding STD treatment programs in the past, but it is not clear whether it is continuing to do so.

BOX A4.1

President Bouteflika's Speech on the World AIDS Day 2003

The Algerian President gave a speech on December 1, 2003, to commemorate the World AIDS Day in Algeria. This was the first time the President extensively addressed the issue in Algeria. In his speech, he expressed the country's commitment to tackle HIV/AIDS in a socially and culturally appropriate manner by breaking the silence around the epidemic, raising awareness among the community, mobilizing key stakeholders to fight against HIV/AIDS, and reducing the discrimination and stigma associated with the epidemic. The President underlined that:

(i) Breaking the silence around HIV/AIDS and taboos of talking about the epidemic in Algeria and other parts of the world is a crucial step to address the epidemic in an adequate manner;

(ii) Raising awareness and HIV-related education, especially among the youth, are important preventive methods in the fight against the spread of HIV/AIDS;

(iii) Women's physiological and social vulnerability to HIV/AIDS is a challenge that needs to be tackled to stem the increasing spread of the epidemic among women;

(iv) Confidentiality must be guaranteed/reinforced in medical centers for voluntary testing to reduce/mitigate people's fear of discrimination and stigma of being exposed as HIV-positive and avoiding testing and treatment;

(v) HIV/AIDS has to be addressed in a socially and culturally appropriate manner, with consideration of local beliefs, values, and traditions to have effective programs to prevent the spread of the epidemic; and

(vi) Collaboration and partnership of different stakeholders, including civil society, the private sector and international agencies is crucial in the fight against HIV/AIDS.

Source: Présidence de la République, www.presidence.dz, December 2003.

In *the Arab Republic of Egypt,* the government program has been largely dependent on outside funding sources. Recently, a situational assessment was completed, and there are plans to develop an NSP. The Ford Foundation has contributed by establishing a hotline, which has been important even if slowly used. Caritas, an NGO, operates a hotline in Alexandria. The Swiss government funds the improvement of blood banks. Small efforts at research into men who have sex with men (MSM) and injecting drug users (IDUs) have been mounted, but neither real outreach programs nor behavioral surveillance has been developed. Through

Family Health International's (FHI) IMPACT program, the United States Agency for International Development (USAID) has begun a local program funded at approximately $1 million yearly. Its first accomplishment was a sexually transmitted infection (STI) study among high-risk groups, carried out in 2000–01. Since then it has helped to develop a voluntary counseling and training (VCT) service; conducted training for health workers on sexually transmitted diseases (STDs), HIV treatment, and blood safety; and is planning to work on improved surveillance, building capacity in community-based organizations (CBOs) that work with IDUs, and reducing stigma. The Ford Foundation, USAID, and the World Health Organization (WHO) contribute to an infectious disease surveillance system and education program through the U.S. Naval Medical Research Unit-3 (NAMRU-3) for HIV, hepatitis C, and hepatitis B. USAID also funds the Center for Development and Population Activities (CEDPA) to work on HIV and STDs with young women in Upper Egypt. The potential for HIV to spread through a significant number of refugees from the Horn of Africa as well as the large number of migrating Egyptians has not yet been addressed. Programs to reduce risk among the most vulnerable groups have not been established.

The Islamic Republic of Iran appears to have the most focused prevention activities composed of a continuum of harm reduction and care for IDUs, including those in prison, with options for treatment of addiction, including methadone maintenance. The interventions being implemented in prisons are innovative and could provide a model for the region (see box A4.2). Plans are under way to provide outreach prevention services to sex workers as well. Public campaigns have begun to alert the general population. The Red Crescent of the Islamic Republic of Iran has mobilized 1 million volunteers to help disseminate its HIV/AIDS anti-stigma message. The programming was launched across all 28 branches of the national organization. Local television advertisements advise the use of condoms and campaign against the isolation of and discrimination against AIDS victims. Couples engaged to be married are required by law to attend HIV/AIDS awareness classes before their marriage. Free (government-financed) needles are distributed at pharmacies to prevent transmission through needle sharing among IDUs. The Islamic Republic of Iran has been approved to receive grants from the GFATM in the last two application rounds of 2002 and 2003. The first two-year grant for $9,698,000 is to improve HIV/AIDS surveillance, raise awareness about the epidemic, and improve access to and quality of HIV/AIDS treatment and care, while the second grant for $5,698,000 is to build the capacity of civil societies in the Islamic Republic of Iran to confront the epidemic.

Jordan has also been successful at receiving approval for a grant from the GFATM for $2,483,900 to conduct a wide range of activities, including targeted interventions with high-risk groups, STI/HIV/AIDS education in schools, establishing VCT centers and promoting their use, providing home-based care and antiretroviral therapy (ART) for all those in need, developing improved surveillance, conducting safe injecting and blood safety assessments, and improving capacity among staff. In addition, FHI has a program in Jordan funded by USAID, at approximately $400,000 per year that has conducted research, designed and implemented an STI prevalence study in the general population, and developed a hotline and counseling center. Peer education activities with out-of-school youth have been developed through UNAIDS Program Acceleration Funds (PAF). Few local NGOs have yet to become involved and capacity to reach and work with vulnerable groups remains limited.

Lebanon has recently been supported by UNAIDS and the Bank in preparing their comprehensive National AIDS Action Plan for 2004–09 to guide leaders and stakeholders in the organization of appropriate interventions

---

BOX A4.2

Islam and Harm Reduction in the Islamic Republic of Iran

With exposure to the issues surrounding HIV among IDUs, the religious leaders in Iran have come to believe that harm reduction is necessary and acceptable in Islam to protect society from the even greater consequence of HIV. Based on their opinions, implementing agencies can carry out such activities as condom distribution and methadone maintenance therapy. Recently, the Islamic Republic of Iran's Prison Organization has obtained permission to start pilot projects on the effectiveness of needle exchanges in prisons to reduce the transmission of HIV. Condoms are already available in prisons because of the establishment of "private meetings" for married couples. There are suites constructed in all prisons for married couples to meet in private, where condoms are provided. HIV prevention training is also provided to all prisoners and their families several times during the period of their imprisonment. The "private meetings" have been very effective in reducing violence and all antisocial behavior. These are considered to be the right of the prisoner and not just a privilege.

Sources: F. Soltani, United Nations Office on Drugs and Crime, Iran and Dr. Ashfar, Prison Organization, personal communication.

that would lead to a coherent and coordinated HIV/AIDS response at the national level. Additional funds from UNAIDS and funds provided by the United Nations Population Fund (UNFPA) through the Organization of the Petroleum Exporting Companies (OPEC) fund, has enabled selected NGOs to undertake behavior surveys and outreach among high-risk groups, such as CSWs, IDUs, and MSM. The action plan has four major priorities: (1) advocacy, human rights, and coordination; (2) prevention; (3) treatment, care, and support; and (4) surveillance and M&E. An operational manual to guide the implementation of the National Plan has recently been completed. The World Bank has also recently approved an Institutional Development Fund Grant of US$350,000 to the Government of Lebanon to support the strengthening of the National HIV/AIDS M&E and Surveillance Systems.

Morocco developed, with technical assistance supported by the Bank, a situational assessment and National AIDS Action Plan, the formulation of which was funded by UNAIDS. This plan was finalized in September 2001 and the government organized a national workshop for its presentation to main stakeholders. The response analysis showed a substantial gap between available and required financial resources. Of the $20 million budget for 2002–04, only 25 percent was available from government resources. With this plan, Morocco developed a successful GFATM proposal and was the first MENA country to receive approval in 2002 for a GFATM grant of $4,738,806 over two years. The proposal targets vulnerable at-risk groups; implements a social communication program aimed at young people, women, and the general population; and provides diagnosis, support, and treatment for people living with HIV/AIDS. There is strong political commitment, evidenced by the financial participation of the government, the help of a few donors such as the European Union and Deutsche Gesellschaft for Technische Zusammenarbeit (GTZ), and collaboration with NGOs.

In *the West Bank and Gaza* there is a small STD/HIV/AIDS program with links to the National Five-Year Health Program. Cases of HIV/AIDS have been detected in Palestinian refugees in Jordan, Lebanon, and Syria, as well as the West Bank and Gaza, and specially designed prevention and care programs are needed, but as yet none have been designed or funded.

In 2002–03, the *Republic of Yemen* developed a strategic framework on HIV/AIDS, and a multisectorial task force has been established to coordinate and oversee the implementation of the NSP. Currently, operational plans are being finalized. In addition, resources have been obtained through the GFATM, bilateral funding, and UN agencies. Despite the challenges that remain in all areas of prevention, care, and support, some attempts now are being made to undertake research and develop programs for risk groups, such as CSWs.

Other nations in the region also have HIV-related activities. For example, Oman is implementing a project with a hotline, Web site, and VCT services for young people; Syria is developing approaches to target youth in slum areas through community-based HIV/AIDS education and communication activities and has received PAF funds from UNAIDS to conduct assessments with the more vulnerable groups in those slums; Tunisia has engaged in HIV/AIDS/STD information, education, and communication campaigns for young people. Libya has begun to address the high risk among IDUs. A rapid assessment and response study is under way and there are plans to improve addiction treatment services.

Status of Program Acceleration Funds 2002–03 in MENA, November 2003

- Twelve countries in MENA have received Program Acceleration Funds (PAF) for a total amount of $791,000. The funds earmarked per country range between a minimum of $30,000 and a maximum of $180,000.

- Three-fourths of the total funds allocated for the MENA region have now been obligated to specific activities, while proposals have been formulated by the countries for the use of the remaining fourth. Because many of these activities were developed in 2003, implementation is ongoing. In 2004, new PAF became available for 2004–05.

- The activities submitted for PAF funding in MENA for 2002–03 were quite wide-ranging and can be regrouped under the following headlines according to those most frequently requested: (1) reinforcing HIV/AIDS prevention work in diverse non-health sectors, including with religious leaders, interior and defense sectors, prisons, and in the workplace; (2) working with specific vulnerable populations, including young people, drug users, sex workers, and so on; (3) support to the National Strategic Planning (NSP) process; (4) capacity building among NGOs and persons living with HIV/AIDS; (5) strengthening information systems, documentation, and best practices; and (6) supporting specific interventions, such as sexually transmitted infections (STI) and epidemiological surveillance. It should be noted that requests from the last category (6) are, and should increasingly become, less frequent as more funds become available to support such key HIV/AIDS interventions through resources available to the UN agencies themselves.

- The following cosponsors have been involved in the implementation of PAF proposals in countries with national counterparts: the World Health Organization, United Nations Children's Fund, United Nations Development Programme, United Nations Office on Drugs and Crime, United Nations Population Fund, and the International Labour Organization.

Source: UNAIDS 2003.

Candidate Countries for the Bank's Support

Countries Ranked by Adult HIV Prevalence Rates[a]	Adult HIV Prevalence Rates (UNAIDS/WHO end of 2003)	GFATM Resources	Ongoing Bank Projects/ Dialogue	National HIV/AIDS Strategic Plans	Other Considerations	Total Score
1. **Djibouti**	**2.9**	**Y**	**Y**	**Y**	**Ongoing HIV/AIDS project and IDA eligible**	**4**
2. West Bank and Gaza	1.6	N	Y	N	Ongoing Conflict	2
3. Algeria	0.1	Y	N	Y	N	2
4. **Morocco**	**0.1**	**Y**	**Y**	**Y**	**Previous Bank assistance on NSP development**	**4**
5. **Yemen, Republic of**	**0.1 (2004)**	**Y**	**Y**	**Y**	**IDA eligible**	**4**
6. Egypt, Arab Rep. of	< 0.1	N	Y	N	NSP under preparation	2
7. **Iran, Islamic Rep. of**	**< 0.1**	**Y**	**Y**	**Y**	**Injecting drug use driving the epidemic**	**4**
8. Iraq	< 0.1	N	Y	N	Ongoing conflict	2
9. **Jordan**	**< 0.1**	**Y**	**Y**	**N**	**Invited Bank to join UNAIDS Theme Group and participate in regular meetings**	**3**
10. **Lebanon**	**0.09**	**N**	**Y**	**Y**	**Previous Bank assistance on NSP development; Requested Bank assistance through IDF grant**	**3**
11. Tunisia	0.06	N	Y	N	N	1
12. Syrian Arab Rep.	0.01	N	N	N	N	0

Note: IDA, International Development Association; IDF, Institutional Development Fund; N, no; NSP, National Strategic Plan; UNAIDS, Joint United Nations Program on HIV/AIDS; Y, yes.

a. Countries listed according to their adult HIV prevalence rates (2003). Countries selected for support have a score of at least 3 and are highlighted in bold face type.

Index